Church and Empire

Church and Empire

Maria E. Doerfler, volume editor;
George Kalantzis, series editor

Fortress Press
Minneapolis

CHURCH AND EMPIRE

Cover image: Ravenna mosaic/Photo: Will Bergkamp

Cover design: Laurie Ingram

Library of Congress Cataloging-in-Publication Data

Print ISBN: 978-1-4514-9635-2

eBook ISBN: 978-1-5064-1693-9

The paper used in this publication meets the minimum requirements of American National Standard for Information Sciences — Permanence of Paper for Printed Library Materials, ANSI Z329.48-1984.

Manufactured in the U.S.A.

This book was produced using Pressbooks.com, and PDF rendering was done by PrinceXML.

Contents

Series Foreword

In his book *The Spirit of Early Christian Thought*, Robert Louis Wilken reminds us that "Christianity is more than a set of devotional practices and a moral code: it is also a way of thinking about God, about human beings, about the world and history" (xiii). From its earliest times, Wilken notes, Christianity has been inescapably ritualistic, uncompromisingly moral, and unapologetically intellectual.

Christianity is deeply rooted in history and continues to be nourished by the past. The ground of its being and the basis of its existence are the life of a historic person, Jesus of Nazareth, whom Christians identify as God's unique, historical act of self-communication. Jesus presented himself within the context of the history of the people of Israel and the earliest disciples understood him to be the culmination of that history, ushering in a new chapter in God's ongoing engagement with the world.

The crucial period of the first few centuries of Christianity is known as the Patristic era or the time of the church fathers. Beginning after the books of the New Testament were written and continuing until the dawn of the Middle Ages (c. 100–700 CE), this period encompasses a large and diverse company of thinkers and personalities. Some came from Greece and Asia

Minor, others from Palestine and Egypt, and still others from Spain, Italy, North Africa, Syria, and present-day Iraq. Some wrote in Greek, others in Latin, and others in Syriac, Coptic, Armenian, and other languages.

This is the period during which options of belief and practice were accepted or rejected. Christian teachers and thinkers forged the language to express Christian belief clearly and precisely; they oversaw the life of the Christian people in worship and communal structure, and clarified and applied the worshiping community's moral norms.

Every generation of Christians that has reconsidered the adequacy of its practice and witness and has reflected seriously on what Christians confess and teach has come to recognize the church fathers as a precious inheritance and source for instruction and illumination. After the New Testament, no body of Christian literature has laid greater claim on Christians as a whole.

The purpose of this series is to invite readers "to return to the sources," to discover firsthand the riches of the common Christian tradition and to gain a deeper understanding of the faith and practices of early Christianity. When we recognize how Christian faith and practices developed through time we also appreciate how Christianity still reflects the events, thought, and social conditions of this earlier history.

Ad Fontes: Sources of Early Christian Thought makes foundational texts accessible through modern, readable English translations and brief introductions that lay out the context of these documents. Each volume brings together the best recent scholarship on the topic and gives voice to varying points of view to illustrate the diversity of early Christian thought. Entire writings or sections of writings are provided to allow the reader to see the context and flow of the argument.

Together, these texts not only chronicle how Christian faith and practice came to adopt its basic shape, but they also summon contemporary readers to consider how the events, insights, and social conditions of the early church continue to inform Christianity in the twenty-first century.

George Kalantzis
Series Editor

Introduction

The thirteenth chapter of John's Apocalypse describes the rise of a progression of horrifying beasts bearing multiple heads, horns, and crowns. These beasts blaspheme God, worship a creature the author describes as "the dragon," and prey upon the church and her saints with a monstrous power and appetite. Like much of Revelation, these passages speak in riddles, appealing to those who have understanding or wisdom to make sense of them. As such, the beasts and their various appendages have long been a source of speculation for readers and students of the New Testament. Hypotheses abound about the institutions or individuals they represent, as well as about the identities of the beasts' horns. Yet while many different theories have been proposed, scholars commonly identify these nightmarish creatures with one or another group of Roman emperors, the rulers and representatives of the empire in which John and most ancient Christians lived. John and his audience evidently experienced these emperors and the Roman authorities at large as blaspheming God and Christ, and as persecuting God's followers. The only hope for relief and vindication for the saints, Revelation suggests, was to suffer on the Lamb's behalf, and await Christ's triumphant return.

John's vision of empire proved persuasive to many Christians, both in his own era and in subsequent centuries. His is not, however, the New Testament's only presentation of civil government. Paul, in the thirteenth chapter of his epistle to the Romans, for example, describes the same emperors John depicts worshiping the dragon as established by God. Whereas in Revelation the empire and its representatives terrorize all Christians, in Romans these authorities hold terror only for those who have done wrong. Whatever right relationship with empire for Christians might mean to the author of Revelation, it must certainly involve deep skepticism and perseverance in Christ even in the face of grave persecution. Romans, by contrast, calls Christians to right relationship with empire by paying, quite literally, their dues, expecting the repayment of good for good and evil for evil, and giving governing authorities honor—if not the honor reserved for Christ. As in the case of Revelation, many Christians in both the first and later centuries found persuasive the vision presented in Romans 13 and 1 Peter 2 for dealing with government.

The tensions between these texts, already evident in the New Testament corpus, prefigure early Christians' ambivalent relationship with empire and government. The history of the Church's relationship with the governing authorities, in other words, unfolds from its very beginnings at the fraught intersection of apprehension and acceptance, collaboration and separation, Revelation 13 and Romans 13. Different eras and different aspects of the tradition emphasize one or the other trajectory, at times embracing civil authority with considerable enthusiasm, at others rejecting its imposition on Christian lives and teachings as hostile or even demonic. Neither voice, however, was ever fully silenced.

This volume is dedicated to helping students chart the

complex, challenging, and challenged narrative that emerges from them in the first six centuries of the Common Era. To divide up this period into a progression of epochs is not without challenges; the process of Christianization and the response to the spread of Christianity by governing authorities progressed at different paces in different parts of the ancient world. From its origins in the Roman province of Judea, Christianity spread across the Roman and the neighboring Sassanid (Persian) empires. By the end of the sixth century, moreover, the Christian presence had long spread into other parts of the world as well, each presenting different contextual challenges in Christians' relations with civic leaders. Such diversity notwithstanding, we may nevertheless identify a general trend by which Christianity throughout the first few centuries of the Common Era gradually moved from the margins of these empires into their very center. The primary sources selected here track these developments, even if they do so in what is by necessity a piecemeal fashion.

The very end of the early Christian era, the sixth and seventh centuries, also marks the rise of Islam. The latter is of great relevance to both the development of Christianity and to Christians' relationship with empire and civil authorities. Living under Muslim rule presented new challenges for churches, many of whom had existed for centuries in Christian-dominated territories. Christians in these areas, including particularly Syria and the Greek-speaking East, sought to respond to their changed circumstances in diverse ways. These developments lie beyond the scope of this volume; an appendix at its conclusion nevertheless points interested students to resources for the study of this period, particularly as they concern Christians' efforts to make sense of and engage with the new governing structures.

Voices from the Margins: The Early Centuries of Christian Development

The earliest witnesses to Christians' relationship with their imperial surroundings come from the New Testament itself, including passages like Mark 12:13-17 and its parallels in Matthew and Luke, 1 Pet. 2:13-17, and the two exemplars already discussed here: Romans 13 and Revelation 13. The fledgling faith, by contrast, seems to have made relatively little impression upon the governing authorities and their historians. Tacitus's *Annals,* his account of the history of the Roman Empire during the opening decades of the first century, mention the Emperor Nero's scapegoating of Christians. Nero had punished the Christians of Rome to cover up his plot to burn down the city; the result, Tacitus writes, was a groundswell of popular sympathy, even though neither Tacitus himself nor the Roman populace seem to have been favorably impressed by Christians in general.

It was, however, Tacitus's contemporary, **Pliny the Younger**, who left the most interesting testament to imperial authorities' engagement with Christians. A governor of the Roman province of Bithynia, modern-day Turkey, Pliny encountered Christians when they were pointed out to him by anonymous sources. Upon questioning a few of them, Pliny found them, on the one hand, obligingly open about their liturgical practices, and, on the other, unwilling to renounce their affiliation even on his order. Faced with this refusal, Pliny wrote to the Roman **Emperor Trajan** for advice. Trajan's response elucidates well the interests and commitments of Roman officials for much of the first two or three centuries of the church's development. Christians, the emperor declared, were not to be sought out. To give ear to anonymous denunciation was contrary to the "spirit of the age," according to Trajan. Once a Christian had to be apprehended, moreover, they were to be given every opportunity to recant and participate in the Roman civic cult. If they failed to do so, however, they were to be punished—for their disobedience to imperial orders, if not for their faith.

The ***Acts of the Martyrs of Scili***, the account of a group martyrdom from the later decades of the second century, illustrate what might have occurred before a Roman authority figure like Pliny from the Christian perspective. Unlike other North African martyr-acts, including, for example, the *Martyrdom of Perpetua and Felicitas*, the *Acts* is remarkably brief and spare. The text takes the form of a transcript, recounting the trial of twelve Christians, seven men and five women, before the North African proconsul Saturninus. At the beginning of the document, the group's allegiances have already been established. Saturninus proceeds to exhort the Christians to "return to the Roman rite," by swearing by the genius—that is to say, the guardian spirit—of the emperor. The Christians, in turn, affirm their identity, insist upon their blameless behavior, and reject all opportunity to reconsider. At the trial's conclusion, they are accordingly sentenced to execution and, the author of the *Acts* avers, "crowned with martyrdom."

How might a modern reader make sense of the Roman imperial response to Christian groups in their midst? Our sources bear witness, on the one hand, to a kind of benign indifference toward Christians' beliefs and liturgical practices. On the other hand, however, Christians' insistence on their confessional identity and concomitant refusal to swear by or offer the token sacrifices to the empire's or emperor's guardian spirits drew a sharp and frequently violent response from

Roman authorities. Part of this dynamic has to do with the role religion played in the Roman Empire, which was by and large rather different from its conception in contemporary Western countries, including the United States. Roman authorities' approach to religion centered first on cult, that is to say, religious practice, rather than belief; and second on the empire's pragmatic needs. Part of Roman historians' fundamental assumption was that each people group both had and ought to have its own gods: like laws and land, deities and rites were markers of a people's identity. When a group was conquered by Rome, the latter generally did not seek to put an end to its vanquished foes' religious practices. Rather, Roman strategies sought to make use of such peoples' rites to integrate the newly acquired territories into the Roman Empire both practically, by exploiting existing structures for gathering taxes, and metaphysically, by adding the conquered peoples' gods to the Roman pantheon.

This is not to say that Roman officials gave free reign to all religious practices; mystery cults and other groups that thrived on secrecy or sought to foment rebellion against the empire were sharply censured. Christians, too, may have run afoul of such prohibitions, either by association with Jewish communities, who experienced grave persecution in both Palestine and Egypt during the second century; or, more likely, by virtue of the exclusion of the uninitiated—that is to say, the unbaptized—from the mysteries of the Eucharist. Beyond these imperfect analogies, Christianity may have been largely unintelligible on its own terms in the Roman framework of religious thought; it did not boast any ethnic or territorial affiliation, rather drawing, as the second-century writer Bardaisan proudly announced, its people from all over the world and from all manner of demographics.

Christians' failure to participate in the central civic and religious rites of the Roman Empire no doubt made them suspect to their neighbors; once they had been called before imperial authorities, moreover, their refusal to sacrifice for the good of the empire resulted in their punishment, by flogging and execution, for insubordination. Even in a world as fraught with violence as the Roman Empire, these dramatic displays apparently drew much public attention. Tertullian, a North African writer at the turn of the third century, argued that the very practice of making martyrs ultimately contributed to the spread of the faith: "Because those who see us die, wonder why we do, for we die like the men [e.g., the ancient philosophers] you admire, not like slaves or criminals. And when they find out [why we die], they join us."[1]

The martyrdom of a Christian or a group of Christians, in other words, could generate much public curiosity. Once roused, such inquiries nevertheless called for a persuasive and winsome defense of the faith. The so-called "apologists," Christian writers including many who had benefited from philosophical training, sought to provide such a defense. The resulting genre, the "Christian apology," consists of writings, treatises, and dialogues that elucidate Christianity's practices and commitments. Many of these documents are addressed to imperial authorities—to emperors, governors, and the Roman senate—and purportedly seek to win for Christians the right to freely practice their religion. Accordingly, the apologists frequently depict Christians as model citizens, and their faith as benefiting the empire. That the apologies in question actually reached their addressees is doubtful in the extreme; rather, they were read and copied by Christians, who were no

1. Tertullian, *Apology* 50 (ANF 3.55).

doubt encouraged both by the defense of their tradition and by the affirmation of their continued Roman identity.

A particularly apt example of this genre comes from the pen of **Justin Martyr**, a second-century self-styled Christian philosopher: his ***First Apology***. Some Christians, Justin conceded, acted in morally or even legally offensive fashion, and the Roman authorities were right to punish them. The empire's task, however, was to search out each individual's responsibility rather than treating all identified with the name of Christ as guilty. Indeed, true Christians were *more* likely to follow the laws of the empire, since they conducted themselves in constant awareness of being watched by a divine authority who prized ethical comportment. To illustrate his point, Justin also adduces Jesus' teachings on such matters as speaking the truth, doing no harm to another, and paying taxes with pleasure and punctuality. In short, Justin argues, "to God alone [Christians] render worship, but in other things we gladly serve you, acknowledging you as kings and rulers of men, and praying that with your kingly power you be found to possess also sound judgment."[2]

Justin's appeals, and those of his fellow apologists, frequently fell on deaf ears, if they reached the ears of imperial authorities at all. Indeed, Justin's by-name—"the Martyr"—suggests just how closely the practice of Christianity's intellectual defense was connected to the willingness to suffer for one's convictions. Yet the assertion that Christianity was wholly compatible with citizenship in the empires of this world, if only those empires were prepared to recognize it as such, sounds prominently in Justin's and his contemporaries' writings. Nor are the sources included here intended to suggest that Christians faced death always and everywhere in the

2. Justin Martyr, *Apology* 17; see *infra* at pp. 11–16.

Roman Empire until the rise of its first Christian emperor, Constantine. Most persecutions were local, instigated either by mob violence or by a local governor. Accordingly, while some parts of the empire generated many martyrs, Christians in other locations lived in a relatively unmolested fashion. It was not until the middle of the third century that an edict by Emperor Decius (201–251 CE) for the first time led to empire-wide persecution of Christians.

The Move toward the Center

The third century was an era of internal and external struggle for the Roman Empire. Civil war, natural disasters and the resulting food shortages, and the constant press against the empire's boundaries by its eastern and northern neighbors all contributed to great instability of imperial leadership: more than twenty emperors succeeded one another in a span of only fifty years. At times, civil authorities sought to remedy the crisis by returning the empire to its religious roots; in 250 CE Decius' edict, for example, required all Roman citizens to sacrifice "for the well-being of the empire." The edict neither mentioned nor presumably explicitly targeted Christians, who were still a small minority among the empire's citizens. Yet its impact fell disproportionately on Christians, particularly in parts of the empire like North Africa where the local authorities were prepared to enforce its requirements with recourse to violence if necessary.

The legacy of the martyrs and their commemoration in churches' liturgical calendars notwithstanding, Christians' response to Decius' edict was far from unanimous. Some indeed refused to sacrifice, suffering martyrdom or torture as a result. Others, however, fled, apostasized and in the process joined the "lapsed" (*lapsi*), or sought to devise alternative solutions for themselves and their families. The practice of purchasing for oneself a so-called "*libellus*," a slip of parchment attesting that one had indeed sacrificed, was sufficiently common to generate grave challenges for the church in the aftermath of the persecution. Christians had traditionally regarded apostasy, along with murder and adultery, to be among the sins that could be forgiven only by God, not, however, by God's worldly representatives. How then were the churches to deal with the large numbers of repentant Christians who had sacrificed or had dealt with persecution in other dishonorable ways?

Moreover, some of those who had succumbed were bishops of large and populous congregations. If such a one had abandoned his see, as had been the case, for example, with Cyprian of Carthage, and another bishop had been named in his place, a church might find itself in involuntary schism upon the original bishop's return. Churches, both individually and in conversation with other congregations, sought to answer all of these questions once enforcement of the edict had ceased. The Decian persecution, in other words, proved remarkably fruitful by generating a new crop of martyrs and "confessors"—those Christians who had stood up under torture but had survived the persecution; it also, however, forced churches to address a series of new theological and practical challenges.

Both developments contributed to the church's considerable growth in the second half of the third century. By the century's end, as many as 10 percent of the empire's population may have been Christians. At the beginning of the fourth century, these Christians had to survive one more persecution under the co-Emperors Diocletian and Galerius. This final persecution was by far the bloodiest, and reflected for the first time an empire-wide, targeted effort to return Christians, at least in their practices, to the Roman religious fold. With Diocletian's retirement from the imperial throne in 305 CE, efforts to enforce the various anti-Christian edicts flagged, and Diocletian's co-emperor in the East, Galerius, by 311 CE, on his deathbed, indeed revoked persecution efforts entirely, permitting Christians to practice their religion freely in his territories.

The true turning point from the perspective of Christian historiography, however, came with the rise of Constantine to leadership of the empire. Constantine had been raised as the son of the Christian Empress Helena, the wife of Constantius, one of the co-emperors during the first decade of the fourth century. Diocletian had sought to break the chain of imperial power from father to son by dividing the empire into four parts, and having each emperor select a successor on the basis of ability and experience instead. These reforms were short-lived: both Constantius' son and the son of his eastern co-emperor sought to become their fathers' successors. After a series of complicated military maneuvers, Constantine indeed successfully established himself as ruler over, first, the Western parts, and, in 324 CE, the entirety of the Roman Empire.

One of Constantine's first actions as (co-)emperor involved officially ending the persecution of Christians across Roman territories. In 313 CE, Constantine and Licinius, Constantine's eastern colleague, co-authored the so-called "**Edict of Milan.**"[3]

3. As contemporary scholars have noted, this label is a wholesale misnomer. Imperial orders in Roman law took many different forms, and the letter authored by the two co-emperors "near Milan" was certainly no edict. The designation has nevertheless proved pervasive, and students are still likely to encounter the document by this moniker in textbooks, popular writings, or even in serious historical scholarship. In the absence of clear and helpful alternatives, this volume retains the older (if somewhat misleading) name.

This law, for the first time, explicitly granted Christians and other citizens of the empire the right to observe the religion of their choosing. The freedom granted was indeed new—and, in the aftermath of the persecution that had characterized the first decade of the fourth century, welcomed as a quasi-miraculous intervention. The law's form and justification, however, anchor the law firmly in the Roman Empire's conception of religion and the nature of the divine. The emperors accordingly granted these freedoms "so that any divinity whatsoever in the seat of the heavens may be propitious and kindly disposed to [the emperors] and all who are placed under our rule." Efforts to maximize divine support for the empire and its rulers, in other words, carried over into this first and most important legal recognition of Christians' freedom to practice their faith.

Tensions between Constantine's celebrated persona as the Roman Empire's first Christian leader and his beholdenness to the forms and ideals of Roman religion continued throughout his reign. Questions concerning Constantine's piety—the genuine nature of his faith—are, for obvious reasons, beyond the scope of historical inquiry. Like his famous vision at the Milvian Bridge, a vision recounted somewhat differently by different Christian historians, Constantine's own religious experience remains, to modern readers, a little out of focus. What we *can* say with confidence is that Constantine took seriously his role as Christianity's benefactor: there are many churches and other Christian edifices among the building projects he initiated throughout his reign. Most prominent among these is the *Anastasis*, the Church of the Resurrection, built at the putative site of Christ's tomb in Jerusalem. Indeed, Constantine's investment in the sites of Jesus' ministry put Jerusalem back onto the Christian map for the first time in centuries: pilgrims flocked to the city to walk where Jesus had walked, and by the end of the fourth century, the site had become a significant focal point of monastic activity as well.

In this as in other things, Constantine both seems to have regarded himself and was evidently regarded by Roman Christians as an important mediator for questions of Christian practice and doctrine. Wherever conflict broke out between different groups of Christians, as, for example, in the case of intra-Christian disagreements over the relationship between Christ and the Father, bishops and other Christian leaders wrote to Constantine for resolution. Still more remarkably, the emperor took their requests seriously, hearing appeals, convening synods, including the first ecumenical council at Nicaea, and sending hortatory letters in pursuit of Christian unity.

Such actions on the part of a civic leader who, like Constantine, until the very end of his life had not even undergone baptism strike contemporary readers as baffling. In the context of the Roman Empire, however, Constantine's interventions were readily intelligible exercises of the emperor's role as *pontifex maximus*, the empire's high priest. Historically, the emperor had served as the empire's religious representative before divine and human audiences. In this vein, heads of the Roman Empire had long worn the mantle of its high priest, and Constantine's shift in religious allegiance from the Roman gods to the Christian God did little to change his and his people's sense that metaphysical and practical responsibility for the empire's well-being were both intricately intertwined and vested in the person of the emperor. This expectation, moreover, carried over into Constantine's successors, and remained prominent well into the empire's Byzantine period.

That Christians experienced the ascendancy of the first Christian emperor as a great boon or even a divinely ordained blessing is easy to understand. Over the course of a scant few years, Roman Christians had gone from witnessing Diocletian's great persecution to enjoying favored status in Constantine's empire. **Eusebius of Caesarea**, one of Christianity's earliest historians and author of the altogether enthusiastic ***Life of Constantine***, depicted his contemporaries' experience as follows:

> All fear therefore of those who had formerly afflicted them was taken away from men, and they celebrated splendid and festive days. Everything was filled with light, and those who before were downcast beheld each other with smiling faces and beaming eyes. With dances and hymns, in city and country, they glorified first of all God the universal King, because they had been thus taught, and then the pious emperor with his God-beloved children.[4]

This passage, taken from the very conclusion of Eusebius' *Ecclesiastical History*, allows readers a glimpse into changing conceptions of how church and empire were to relate to one another. After centuries of tribulation, Eusebius argued, Christ had delivered Christians safely into the hands of one of their own. What remained to be done for Christians except to rejoice and embrace him?

The confidence Eusebius expresses in Constantine as Christ's chosen messenger and the climax of a divine plan to show favor to the Christians of the empire would not last. After Constantine's death in 337 CE, the empire was divided between his three sons, all of whom were Christians, even if not all agreed to the Nicene formula—the confession that Christ shared the Father's very essence—that had been brokered

4. Eusebius, *Hist. eccl.* 10.9.7.

under their father's guidance. By 361 CE, however, all three had been killed in battle, to be succeeded by Constantine's nephew Julian. The latter, despite his Christian upbringing, had come to reject Christianity in favor of a philosophically accented affirmation of the old Roman gods. He did not persecute Christians like some of his pagan forebears, but sought to hinder the religion's spread by other means, removing imperial funding for Christian building projects, recalling from exile bishops who had been sent there under his predecessors, and, perhaps most troublingly for Christian authors, limiting the upper echelons of rhetorical education to those who held to the Roman religion. The literary backlash against Julian was predictably swift and vicious; at the end of his brief reign, Christian authors celebrated his death in battle as God's comeuppance against "the Apostate."

Ephrem, the most important author and theologian of Syriac literature in the fourth century, composed four ***Hymns against Julian***, of which only the third is reproduced here. In it, he recounts the raising of the Persian flag over Nisibis in the aftermath of Julian's defeat, at the same time as the dead emperor's body was being brought into the city. The loss of Nisibis to the Sassanians meant that the city was now officially under Zoroastrian power. In Ephrem's assessment, however, the loss for the Roman army was a just punishment for Julian's apostasy: God had made an exemplar of the proud emperor by contrasting his ineffectual corpse with the divine power and saving grace of the crucified one Julian had mocked.

Ephrem's hymn is a stark reminder that not all of Rome's neighbors had embraced or even sanctioned Christianity at the same time. Indeed, the more firmly the Roman Empire came to be identified with the Christian religion, the more suspicious neighboring peoples became of the Christians in their midst. Yet Christ was not bound to any particular people, Ephrem argued, and could make use even of an empire that sheltered comparatively few Christian converts to chastise a Roman leader's theological missteps. Julian's successors would all be Christians, even if they did not necessarily adhere to Nicene orthodoxy. With the death of Julian, however, Constantine's imperial line had come to an end: Eusebius' predictions of an empire preserved by God for the pious emperor and his offspring forever had proved false mere decades after his and Constantine's deaths.

Christianity at the Heart of the Empire

Roman emperors, in their dealings with the empire's religious groups, could draw upon a wide range of tools: their ability to grant and withhold funds; their use of personal appeals and moral suasion; even their presence at key ecclesiastical events could give voice to a civic leader's desires. An emperor's most common strategy for engaging with his people involved the Roman legal apparatus. From Constantine's reign on, Christians appealed to Roman authorities for legal resolution of various dilemmas: a priest might feel unduly burdened by civic obligations, an influx of monks might prove a nuisance for a city, and, perhaps most notably, one group of Christians might judge another guilty of heresy and of impeding the spread and practice of the true faith.

The ***Theodosian Code***, a compendium of Roman laws assembled in the middle of the fifth century under the auspices of Theodosius II, contains legal provisions for all of these scenarios and many more. Indeed, the entirety of the *Code*'s Book 16 is dedicated to religious matters, and covers legislation from the beginnings of the fourth century all the way through

Theodosius II's own era. Nor are these all the laws, edicts, and rescripts dealing with matters of religion produced by Roman emperors in these decades; the jurists responsible for the *Code*'s composition—an unprecedented effort in Roman history—exercised a measure of discretion in their selection, in the process undoubtedly omitting many laws. This volume reproduces only a small selection of the *Theodosian Code*'s provisions concerning Christianity. Each law is marked by the date and the emperors responsible for it.

Roman law wove a pervasive red thread through the religious lives of the empire's citizens. Constantine had publicly sanctioned the practice of the Christian faith in 313 CE. Not quite seventy years later, in 380 CE, Theodosius and his co-emperors went a step further, establishing Christianity as Rome's official religion (*Codex Theodosianus* 16.1.2). Those Christians whose faith conformed to Damasus and Peter, bishops of Rome and Alexandria, respectively, were to be known as "catholic," a term meaning "all-encompassing" or "worldwide." Those who did not so identify—and there were many—the law declared heretics, and threatened with swift retribution by both God and the emperor.

Further, more targeted laws would soon substantiate Theodosius' and his co-emperors' ominous warnings. Even prior to Christianity's establishment as the empire's religion, Roman laws intervened authoritatively in the religious lives of its citizens. In the 350s, a series of laws requiring the closure of pagan temples and prohibiting access to them canvassed the empire (*Codex Theodosianus* 16.10.4), although the traditional Roman festivals, many of which were linked to cultic activity, continued (*Codex Theodosianus* 16.10.17). The same period saw the publication of a law stripping Christians who had converted to Judaism of all their property (*Codex Theodosianus*

16.8.7). Moreover, Christians who apostacized—who abandoned Christian faith and practice—lost the ability to make a will or to inherit from anyone (*Codex Theodosianus* 16.7.1). On occasion, the law even regulated the sacramental mode of entry into the faith, baptism. To be more precise, it endowed with imperial force orthodox bishops' resolution that there was to be no re-baptism (*Codex Theodosianus* 16.6.2). By valorizing single baptism as both normative and lawful, the emperors penalized other Christian groups' attempts to initiate new converts. Roman law, in other words, sought to police the boundaries between different religious groups, making entry into catholic Christianity easy and access to alternative religious practices costly or outright illegal.

The latter applied with additional force to heretical variants of Christianity. The lengthy section of the *Code* dedicated to laws against various heresies suggests the ever-growing number of, in Theodosius' words, "insane" or "demented" Christians (cf. *Codex Theodosianus* 16.1.2). One edict will suffice to illustrate emperors' efforts to establish Christian orthodoxy. *Codex Theodosianus* 16.5.38, handed down by the co-emperors Arcadius, Honorius, and Theodosius in 404 CE, directs itself against Manicheans, a religious offshoot from Christianity, and Donatists, North African Christians who had lived in schism from the Church catholic in that part of the empire for nearly a century. The religion of the empire, the law suggests, was to be harmonious, just as there was harmony in the Godhead. Those who sought to introduce disharmony and diversity into this unity would be punished by the provisions, in 405 already numerous, against heretics. Indeed, the law explicitly anticipated and sought to discourage these groups' attempts to rise up against imperial authority: "If perchance seditious mobs should assemble, [the heretic] shall not doubt that the sharp goads of a more severe punishment will be applied to him." Those who did not hold to the pro-Nicene (and later pro-Chalcedonian) faith could suffer gravely for their heretical views: the *Code* contemplates their being driven out of cities, particularly Rome and Constantinople; their loss of property; reassignment of that property to catholic Christians; and even their loss of life. These laws, where enforced, undoubtedly presented strong incentives to cast one's lot with catholic Christianity, particularly since those who were prepared to (re-)embrace the pro-Nicene faith were rewarded with the emperors' immediate pardon (*Codex Theodosianus* 16.5.41).

These laws suggest that, even several generations after Constantine's reign, the Christianization of the Roman Empire remained a gradual process. Nevertheless, by the latter half of the fourth century, the tables had noticeably turned. During the first centuries of the Common Era, Christian apologists had sought to make their faith and practice palatable to Roman authorities, or at least those concerned about the compatibility of their civil and religious allegiances. Now, by contrast, pagan writers tried to make the case for the continuation of Greco-Roman rites as part of the empire's grand heritage. In the Greek East, **Libanius**, a famous teacher of rhetoric who had trained both Christian and non-Christian students in the art of public speaking, appealed to Emperor Theodosius for protection of the pagan temples. Christian monks, Libanius writes, had resorted to unauthorized self-help in removing these edifices, destroying in many cases ancient and beautiful buildings in the name of their religion. Yet conversion, Libanius pointedly reminded his audience, depended not on the destruction of temples, but on the changing of hearts. It was there that Christians had fallen short: many of those whom Christians considered to be among their ranks were merely pretending to have abandoned their former rites: "[Many of the Christians'] converts have not really been changed—they only say they have. This does not mean that they have exchanged one faith for another—only that this crew have been bamboozled. They go to their ceremonies, join their crowds, go everywhere these do, but when they adopt an attitude of prayer, they either invoke no god at all or else they invoke the gods."[5]

In the West, too, the question of Christianity's coexistence with Greco-Roman cult remained a point of debate. **Ambrose, bishop of Milan** at the end of the fourth century, and **Symmachus**, a Roman senator and Prefect of the City of Rome, accordingly vied for Emperor Valentinian's favor concerning the altar of the goddess Victory. The latter had stood on the steps of the Roman senate building for centuries, and had been a locus for the swearing of oaths. Emperor Gratian had removed the altar and had similarly withdrawn fiscal support from the Vestal Virgins, an ancient order of priestesses whose cult had been central to Roman identity from its very origins. The old gods, Symmachus argued, had served Rome well; their worship had been vindicated by great military triumphs. Ought the emperors, so recently converted to the new religion, Christianity, do away with tradition entirely? Did not all faiths alike ultimately seek after truth? "We [the pagan Roman senators] ask," Symmachus writes, "for peace for the gods of our fathers and of our country. It is just that all worship should be considered as one. We look on the same stars, the sky is common, the same world surrounds us. What difference does it make by what pains each seeks the truth? We cannot attain to so great a secret by one road; but this discussion is rather for persons at ease; we offer now prayers, not conflict."[6]

5. Libanius, *Oratio* 30.28; see *infra* at pp. 45–56.

Such an argument might well strike contemporary readers as persuasive. Symmachus's Christian contemporaries, however, mindful of the still-recent persecution of Christians and anxious not to lose a foothold in the heart of the empire, disagreed. Rome, its emperors, and many of its people, including a number of its senators, had embraced the truth of the faith, Ambrose argued; how could they now take a step backwards and return to the old evil in violation of their own consciences? Ambrose had even Rome personified speak up against Symmachus's plea: "This alone was common to me with the barbarians, that of old I knew not God. . . . Let God Himself, Who made me, teach me the mystery of heaven, not man, who knew not himself."[7]

That clergy and bishops took the initiative in such high-stakes negotiations need not surprise us. From Constantine's era onward, Roman law also addressed itself to Christian clergy, extending certain benefits particularly to bishops. The latter were exempt from tax payments and from holding certain expensive and time-consuming public offices. Roman law also protected clergy from being sued before an imperial magistrate (*Codex Theodosianus* 16.2.42); those who had undergone ordination, the law suggests, could be judged only by a bishop or, in cases where the accused was himself of the episcopal rank, before a tribunal of bishops. The latter also sat in judgment over matters pertaining to religion (*Codex Theodosianus* 16.11.1), and ordinary citizens could and did appeal to bishops for resolution of their claims. These laws suggest a growing esteem for and public presence of Christian clergy. Not surprisingly, by the second half of the fourth century, even the upper echelons of Roman society began to

6. Symmachus, *Relatio* III.10; see *infra* at pp. 57–64.
7. Ambrose, *Ep.* 72.7; see *infra* at 65–93.

treat these offices as a potentially viable career. One of the earliest instances of this phenomenon in the Latin West was indeed **Ambrose**, already noted above as Symmachus's Christian interlocutor.

The son of a senatorial family, Ambrose had progressed through a series of imperial posts before becoming governor of the Roman province of Liguria in northern Italy. Milan had long been a contested site between different groups of Christians; its bishop, Auxentius, rejected the Nicene formula, but proved sufficiently popular among his own people to resist pro-Nicene Christians' efforts to unseat him. After his death in 374 CE, tensions between the rival Christian groups over who ought to become the next bishop of Milan threatened to turn violent. Ambrose, in his capacity as governor, sought to intercede, only to find himself singled out as the local Christians' consensus candidate for the episcopacy of Milan. Ambrose claims to have resisted their acclamation; despite growing up in a Christian household, he was not yet baptized and lacked the theological training required for the ministry. His civic office, moreover, required compromised purity. The author of Ambrose's ancient biography, Paulinus of Milan, suggests that Ambrose sought to demonstrate his unsuitability, *inter alia*, by sentencing a man to death. Milan's Christians did not relent, and Ambrose in due course submitted to both baptism and ordination. The politically charged atmosphere of his initial appellation, however, foreshadowed a similarly engaged ministry. Ambrose would befriend, confront, and collaborate with several emperors, who would in turn leave their mark upon Christian faith and practice across the Roman Empire.

Milan was the seat of the court for one of Rome's co-emperors throughout parts of the later fourth century. In the

380s CE, the child-emperor Valentinian II (371–392 CE) and his mother, the Empress Justina, were accordingly among Ambrose's spiritual charges. Ambrose had been on good terms with Valentinian II's half-brother, Emperor Gratian, a pro-Nicene Christian; the Empress and her court, however, belonged to the so-called Homoians, Christians who rejected the Nicene formula and consubstantiality of Christ with the Father. They were, in other words, among the heretics that the *Theodosian Code*'s provisions would later seek to curb.

The court and the bishop seem to have coexisted in relative peace for some years; in 386 CE, however, tensions erupted when Valentinian II's representatives sought to requisition for their use—and Homoian practice—one of Milan's basilicas. Ambrose rejected the request out of hand, the court sought to acquire a basilica by force, and in the weeks leading up to Easter, the controversy escalated in a precarious stand-off. Ambrose, in ***Ep.* 75**, depicts himself and his congregation sequestered in the church throughout the night, holding vigil and singing hymns, while the perplexed soldiers stationed at the basilica's doors allowed Christians to enter without, however, allowing any of them to leave.

To contemporary readers the scene appears ripe for slaughter; Ambrose's tenacity—and, the bishop argued, divine blessing—nevertheless carried the day. The emperor withdrew his soldiers and the cathedral remained in pro-Nicene hands for the time being. Ambrose's triumph was nevertheless a qualified one: a year later, Valentinian and his two co-emperors passed an edict sanctioning Homoian worship. In the aftermath of the edict's passage, Gratian, himself a pro-Nicene, requested the use of one of Milan's basilicas for Valentinian II and his court; Ambrose acceded.

As a vocal defender of pro-Nicene Christianity, Ambrose

enjoyed a largely positive relationship with Nicaea's imperial champion, the Emperor Theodosius. Indeed, in his eulogy for Theodosius, Ambrose claimed that the emperor had asked for him repeatedly in his dying hour, with his last breath—a self-serving literary flourish, no doubt, but testimony that Ambrose at least wished to be seen as having been among Theodosius' nearest and dearest. The relationship between the influential bishop and the devout emperor was not, however, without its challenges. Theodosius had inherited an empire fraught with internal and external strife. The threat of civil war loomed large, and Theodosius spent much of his time as emperor quashing rebellions. When a public uprising in a Greek town named Thessaloniki killed, among others, the local governor, Theodosius' representative in the region, the emperor gave his army free rein in retaliation. The result was mass carnage: as many as seven thousand from among the local population were killed.

These consequences, while grave and horrifying to both modern audiences and ancient moralists, were nevertheless well within an emperor's contemplated official duties. Constantine had put off baptism until the point of death, when he was prepared to strip off the imperial purple for good; the brutal nature of a Roman ruler's responsibilities, he felt, was incompatible with baptismal purity. Theodosius, by contrast, had been baptized at the beginning of his reign, albeit during a period of severe illness. As such, his conduct left him open to additional scrutiny from even those ecclesiastics most sympathetic to his reign. When Theodosius traveled to Milan in the aftermath of the Thessaloniki massacre, he did so expecting to have Ambrose celebrate the Eucharist in his presence. Ambrose, however, demurred. In ***Ep.* 37**, he informed the emperor: "I, indeed, though a debtor to your kindness, for which I cannot be ungrateful . . . ; I, I say, have no cause for a charge of stubborn refusal of your request, but have cause for fear. I dare not offer the [eucharistic] sacrifice if you intend to be present." The emperor, Ambrose suggested, had been tainted before God and the Church by his order to put to the sword the people of Thessaloniki. Such an act, if performed by a private individual, would count as murder, a grave sin that would have excluded the unrepentant Christian from participating in the Lord's Supper many times over. Nor did Theodosius' exercise of imperial authority shelter him from living up to his baptismal commitments. "Is what is not allowed when the blood of one innocent victim has been shed, allowed when the blood has been shed of many?" Ambrose asked, and promptly turned to answer his own question: "I do not think so."[8]

For the emperor to be admitted to the eucharistic communion of his fellow Christians at Milan, Ambrose argued, he would have to perform public penance, humbling himself before the entire assembly. The Christian historian Theodoret in his *Ecclesiastical History* portrays Theodosius as gladly acceding to the bishop's demands, and describes the ensuing scenario in dramatic detail: "[The emperor] plucked out his hair; he smote his head; he sprinkled the ground with drops of tears and prayed for pardon. When the time came for him to bring his oblations to the holy table, weeping all the while he stood up and approached the sanctuary."[9]

Even stripped of rhetorical flourishes, the stand-off between Ambrose and Theodosius at the altar is a stunning display of episcopal power. Ambrose's panache is striking: how could a bishop dare? More startling still is Theodosius' response: why

8. *Ep.* 37.13.
9. Theodoret, *Hist. Ecc.* 5.17, translation my own.

would an emperor comply? Part of the answer surely rests with the combination of senatorial prestige, theological pedigree, and personal gravitas that Ambrose brought to the see of Milan. Other bishops, too, sought to appropriate for themselves the role of the prophet—or, in Greco-Roman culture, of the philosopher—vis-à-vis the empire's rulers; few in this early era were as successful as Ambrose: his famous contemporary John Chrysostom, bishop of Constantinople, for example, ran afoul of the eastern court's displeasure and was forced to go into exile.

Dramatic political change overtook the western part of the empire, moreover, just a few short years after Ambrose's death. The Roman Empire's boundaries had always been porous, and the regions closest to them subject to invasions, territorial dispute, and battle. By the beginning of the fifth century, the Germanic tribes that had long dwelled to the North of the Western Roman Empire, compelled in part by the expansion of their own Nordic neighbors, the Huns, began to make inroads into Roman territory. In 410 CE, negotiations between Alaric, the leader of the Visigoths, and the Roman Emperor Honorius broke down, leading Alaric to lay siege to and, in due course, to plunder the city of Rome. In practical terms, the invasion was brief and, by ancient standards, restrained: the Visigoths stripped the city of valuables, killed those who sought to stop them, and, particularly grievously, raped Roman women, including those who had committed themselves to permanent virginity. The invaders, many of whom were themselves Christians, nevertheless did not engage in mass slaughter, respected the city's major basilicas as places of sanctuary, and after only three days moved on to other parts of the Italian peninsula.

The sack of Rome—the first of several—nevertheless exerted

dramatic impact on the imagination of the Empire's citizens. The city that many had thought inviolable had been taken by the enemy, the memorials of its most celebrated leaders stripped, its leading citizens menaced and driven out. This realization shook both Christian Romans and those who continued to adhere to the pagan gods. The latter group evidently attributed the events to the empire's embrace of Christianity and abandonment of the old ways; the gods had shielded Rome as long as Romans were faithful to them, but had abandoned the people in light of their embrace of the Christian religion. Christians, too, harbored doubts: how had God permitted God's own to suffer such losses, and not shielded even the most devoted adherents?

Christian writers sought to address these questions, none more so than **Augustine** of Hippo. By the 410s, Augustine had already been bishop of the North African town of Hippo for over a decade; a former resident of Rome, and, famously, one of Ambrose's catechumens in Milan, Augustine must have shared his contemporaries' initial alarm. Yet, as he maintained in his *magnum opus* ***On the City of God, against the Pagans***, true Christians could only benefit from even the most superficially trying of circumstances. By the loss of property or even life, God tested Christians, proving them either already mature, and as such not attached to the things of this world, or providing them with opportunities for spiritual formation: "Our God is everywhere present, wholly everywhere; not confined to any place. He can be present unperceived, and be absent without moving; when He exposes us to adversities, it is either to prove our perfections or correct our imperfections; and in return for our patient endurance of the sufferings of time, He reserves for us an everlasting reward."[10] The pagan gods, by

10. *De civitate Dei* 1.29.

contrast, had not been able to protect Rome even during the times of the empire's firmest devotion to them, and would be of no use to adherents even in the afterlife, Augustine argued.

Most of *City of God*, however, reflects Augustine's efforts to reformulate Christian ways of thinking about history, and particularly the relationship between God's people, the Church, and worldly powers. Less than a century before, Eusebius had celebrated Constantine's triumphs as divine reward for the emperor's faith—God's pleasure reflected in the military successes of a civic leader. Yet much had changed in the intervening decades. The imperial line, excepting Julian's brief reign, had remained Christian. Their faith, however, had not kept the Visigoths at bay. Nor did it shield North Africa from the influx of the Vandals, another northern tribe who had made their way through Gaul and Spain, and would by the time of Augustine's death go on to conquer Carthage and Hippo as well. Augustine's vision of history and the relationship of Christians to their worldly surroundings accordingly differed dramatically from Eusebius'.

History, Augustine argued, was the unfolding story of two "cities" (Latin: *civitas*, pl. *civitates*), two communities, each of which had a different point of origin, a different destination, and was composed of different constituencies. Most importantly, however, the cities differed in the loves that shaped them: one, the "City of God," was shaped by the love of God, while the other, the "human city," reflected rather a love of self. This love, and the orientation it entails, is the key to understanding each people's nature, beginning, and end. "It is clear that to discover the character of any people we should take a close look at what it loves," Augustine writes.[11] Inhabitants of both cities journeyed alongside one another in

11. *De civitate Dei* 19.24; see *infra* at 93–105.

this world, each *en route* from their primordial origins to their eventual fate. Yet while citizens of the divine city were destined for the heavenly Jerusalem where they would enjoy eternal communion with God, those who belonged to the "city of man" were headed rather to their eternal damnation.

These differences notwithstanding, however, individual members of these cities could be difficult to tell apart in the present age: not all who identified as Christians, Augustine argued, were among the pilgrim people of God, headed for eternal union with the divine. The Church was rather a field on which, as in Matt. 13:24-30, wheat and tares—citizens of both cities—grew alongside one another. At the harvest, the last judgment, God would sort out the two and direct them to their fates. History, by contrast, despite being the territory both cities traversed, was at best a difficult-to-interpret guide to divine favor. It was the mark of a true Christian rather to thrive spiritually in all circumstances than to enjoy tangible rewards this side of the Eschaton—a principle that applied as much to emperors as it did to their lowliest subjects.

Augustine's firm separation of heavenly hope from worldly fate, however, did not suggest that Christians could or even ought to shirk civic responsibilities. Augustine's writings offer ample testimony that he, despite his basically monastic temperament, took seriously the responsibilities of his office, including those that brought him in contact with Roman authorities. Augustine's letters, treatise, and biography show him as a communal leader involved in the daily lives of his people, in adjudicating lawsuits, interceding with Roman governors, and even approving of Roman laws targeting his doctrinal opponents. Indeed, as Roman civic authority receded in North Africa in the face of Vandal invasion, Christian clergy took on additional responsibility for helping order the practical lives of the remaining population.

By the time of Augustine's death in 430 CE, the fall of the Western Roman Empire was still nearly half a century away. The signs of its demise were, however, readily apparent. Both the Byzantine Empire in the East and the various successor kingdoms in the West would, in due course, seek to lay claim to the legacy of the Roman Empire. While both East and West supported a range of approaches to Christians' engagement with civic power, the church's relationship with the governing authorities nevertheless took different turns in each realm.

Trajectories, East and West

The question of when, precisely, the Western Roman Empire "ended" is more difficult to answer than it might at first appear. The deposition of Emperor Romulus Augustus by Flavius Odoacer, the leader of the Germanic tribes, in 476 CE is frequenty treated as the decisive date. The historical reality, however, and the experience of both Christians and non-Christians living in the Latin West, seems to have been a lot less clear. On the one hand, the Eastern Roman Empire recognized both Odoacer and the Gothic king Theodoric who would go on to depose him as viceroys, deputized by the Romans to rule Italy; on the other hand, the territories of the Western Empire had shrunk precipitously throughout the fifth century. The West was rapidly growing fragmented, partitioned between Goths, Franks, Vandals, and various smaller groups, with the Roman East, the Byzantine Empire, retaining at points at least a foothold in the West as well.

Rome, the major episcopal see in Western Europe, during this period was itself caught between the succession of powers warring over Italy. Most of these "barbarian" rulers—that is to say, rulers who came from beyond the Roman territories—were Christians, as were their people, even if not all consented to a pro-Nicene Christianity. Power structures and boundaries in these lands remained in flux for several centuries, presenting ecclesiastical authorities with many practical challenges. During the later medieval period, the church of Rome sought to mitigate the threat of encroaching armies by forming allegiances with different rulers, trading military protection against papal blessing. From particularly the eighth century onward, the church of Rome also established itself as a landholder and, to a more limited extent, military power in its own right. In the final decades of the Western Roman Empire and the aftermath of its demise, however, the relationship between the church and civil authorities was by necessity less intimate than was the case in the Roman East.

The Byzantine Empire had not remained untouched by the processes of northern migration and expansion that had so left their mark on the West: in 443 CE, Emperor Theodosius II had paid a considerable sum to Attila to effect the Huns' withdrawal from his territories. Unlike the West, however, the Byzantine Empire remained unified for another millennium, and Constantinople, its capital and major ecclesiastical see, despite occasional threats remained inviolate. Constantine, the first Christian emperor, had established the city as "a new Rome" more than a century earlier; Constantinople had been the capital city of Christian emperors, even before it became the seat of important bishops and ecclesiastical councils. Christianity accordingly had been woven into its social and political fabric. That Christian faith and civic authority should be particularly intertwined in it and in the Byzantine Empire more broadly is thus perhaps not surprising.

Not all bishops in either East or West acceded readily to this model, particularly insofar as Eastern Roman emperors sought to extend their authority over the church as well. The tension becomes apparent in **Gelasius I**'s famous letter ***Duo sunt*** (trans. "there are two," the opening words of the epistle) to Emperor Anastasius. In it, Gelasius, bishop of Rome from 492 until 496 CE, sought to outline the difference between two kinds of powers: the "holy authority of the priesthood" (*sacrata auctoritas pontificium*), and the "royal power" (*regalis potestas*). The former was the weightier, Gelasius argued, inasmuch as bishops had to give an accounting for even the souls of kings before the heavenly court. Still, bishops submitted to the laws of kings and did not interfere with their civil administration of the government—how much more ought kings submit to the authority of bishops in spiritual and ecclesiastical matters?

Gelasius' letter has frequently been described as setting the tone for Western political theology for centuries to come. Yet it is also of a piece with Gelasius' influential predecessors Ambrose and Augustine. The "balance of powers" on which the letter insists—a balance admittedly weighted toward the ecclesiastical side—also attests to the continued existence of the two poles between which Christians had sought to negotiate their relationship with civil authority from the faith's very beginnings. There is suspicion and apprehension, reflecting perhaps the theological tensions between West and East that had spilled over into the relationship between the western church and the Byzantine Empire in the decades preceding Gelasius' ministry. Yet Gelasius also readily acceded to the royal power being divinely instituted and capable of beneficial collaboration with spiritual authority, just as long as the proper spheres were respected.

Nor is Gelasius' letter the final word on negotiating Christians' relationship with empire. Throughout the history of the church, different voices—each attempting to be faithful to the gospel, the Scriptures, and the best of the church's tradition—emphasized either distance and apprehension, or compliance and collaboration with the governing authorities. With the benefit of hindsight, contemporary readers frequently find it easy to judge one or the other as the right response: Why did medieval Christians living in the so-called Holy Roman Empire not object to the entrenchment between imperial and ecclesial authorities? How could German Christians in the Third Reich have failed to notice the wisdom of Barth, Bonhoeffer, and the Confessing Church?

Contemporary Christians are surely right to reflect critically on the judgments and misjudgments of past eras. Great danger, however, lies in considering oneself and one's own tradition immune to similar mistakes. A study of the Church's relationship with empire ought to enable us rather to think critically about our own context. A sympathetic reading of all aspects of Christian history—that is to say, a reading that aims, first and foremost, to understand and to learn—allows us to practice similar discernment in our own lives and the lives of Christians all over the world today, and to speak to the church's legacy with courage and humility. The question of how Christians ought to relate to empire, or, for that matter, to the nation-state, is far from settled in the twenty-first century. As Christians encounter new political contexts, new challenges, and new opportunities, the Church's tradition and the many voices that contribute to its formation remain a vital resource.

Postscript: Christians and the Rise of Islam

The early decades of the seventh century marked a sea change for Christians across Europe and the Middle East. Muhammad, a new religious and military leader, had succeeded in converting the Arab tribes to monotheism and in leading them in a series of conquests that stunned both Romans and Persians. By the middle of the seventh century, the Sassanid Empire was no more, and the Arab Caliphate encompassed much of North Africa and was making inroads on Byzantine territory. Given such rapid expansion, on the one hand, and eastern Christians' enthusiastic missionary activity, on the other, for a time as many as half of the world's Christians were living under Muslim rule.

These changes presented new challenges for Christians. As "People of the Book" they and their Jewish neighbors enjoyed a measure of protection from Muslim rulers; their status was, however, dependent on Christians' payment of a polltax, and their compliance with restrictions on Christian building activities, evangelism, and other religious practices. In response, Christian writers appropriated a number of ancient literary genres, including the apology and the apocalypse, to fortify churches and discourage believers' conversion to Islam. Christians also began to formulate law for their communities to address concerns and opportunities that arose in their changed environment.

Christians of different traditions, in different areas, at different times, and under different rulers experienced their lives and negotiations with Muslim civil authorities very differently. These developments lie beyond the scope of our volume; they are, however, of great importance to students of Christians' relations with state and empire. Happily, recent years have seen the publication of a number of resources, including both collections and translations of primary sources, and secondary sources designed to contextualize and illuminate these writings. To readers interested in more information of these developments, we particularly commend the publications listed below.

Sourcebooks on Early Muslim/Christian Relations

- Robert Hoyland, *Seeing Islam as Others Saw It: A Survey and Evaluation of Christian, Jewish and Zoroastrian Writings on Early Islam* (Princeton: Darwin, 2014).
- Michael P. Penn, *When Christians First Met Muslims: A Sourcebook of the Earliest Syriac Writings on Islam* (Los Angeles: University of California Press, 2015).
- Jardel Rodriguez, *Muslim and Christian Contact in the Middle Ages: A Reader* (Toronto: University of Toronto Press, 2015).

Texts and Translations

1

Voices from the Margins: The Early Centuries of Christian Development

I. Revelation 13, New Revised Standard Version

1 And I saw a beast rising out of the sea, having ten horns and
seven heads; and on its horns were ten diadems, and on its
heads were blasphemous names. 2 And the beast that I saw was
like a leopard, its feet were like a bear's, and its mouth was
like a lion's mouth. And the dragon gave it his power and his
throne and great authority. 3 One of its heads seemed to have
received a death-blow, but its mortal wound had been healed.
In amazement the whole earth followed the beast. 4 They
worshiped the dragon, for he had given his authority to the
beast, and they worshiped the beast, saying, "Who is like the
beast, and who can fight against it?"

5 The beast was given a mouth uttering haughty and

blasphemous words, and it was allowed to exercise authority
for forty-two months. 6 It opened its mouth to utter
blasphemies against God, blaspheming his name and his
dwelling, that is, those who dwell in heaven. 7 Also it was
allowed to make war on the saints and to conquer them. It
was given authority over every tribe and people and language
and nation, 8 and all the inhabitants of the earth will worship
it, everyone whose name has not been written from the
foundation of the world in the book of life of the Lamb that was
slaughtered.

9 Let anyone who has an ear listen:
10 If you are to be taken captive,
    into captivity you go;
if you kill with the sword,
    with the sword you must be killed.
Here is a call for the endurance and faith of the saints.

11 Then I saw another beast that rose out of the earth; it had
two horns like a lamb and it spoke like a dragon. 12 It exercises
all the authority of the first beast on its behalf, and it makes
the earth and its inhabitants worship the first beast, whose
mortal wound had been healed. 13 It performs great signs, even
making fire come down from heaven to earth in the sight of
all; 14 and by the signs that it is allowed to perform on behalf
of the beast, it deceives the inhabitants of earth, telling them
to make an image for the beast that had been wounded by the
sword and yet lived; 15 and it was allowed to give breath to the
image of the beast so that the image of the beast could even
speak and cause those who would not worship the image of the
beast to be killed. 16 Also it causes all, both small and great,
both rich and poor, both free and slave, to be marked on the
right hand or the forehead, 17 so that no one can buy or sell
who does not have the mark, that is, the name of the beast or

the number of its name. 18 This calls for wisdom: let anyone
with understanding calculate the number of the beast, for it is
the number of a person. Its number is six hundred sixty-six.

II. Rom. 13:1-7, New Revised Standard Version

1 Let every person be subject to the governing authorities; for
there is no authority except from God, and those authorities
that exist have been instituted by God. 2 Therefore whoever
resists authority resists what God has appointed, and those
who resist will incur judgment. 3 For rulers are not a terror
to good conduct, but to bad. Do you wish to have no fear of
the authority? Then do what is good, and you will receive its
approval; 4 for it is God's servant for your good. But if you do
what is wrong, you should be afraid, for the authority does
not bear the sword in vain! It is the servant of God to execute
wrath on the wrongdoer. 5 Therefore one must be subject, not
only because of wrath but also because of conscience. 6 For the
same reason you also pay taxes, for the authorities are God's
servants, busy with this very thing. 7 Pay to all what is due
them—taxes to whom taxes are due, revenue to whom revenue
is due, respect to whom respect is due, honor to whom honor
is due.

III. Correspondence between Pliny and the Emperor Trajan (c. 112 CE)

Pliny the Younger, during his governorship of the Roman province Bithynia-Pontus, modern-day Turkey, encountered a new religious group, the Christians. Those who could claim Roman citizen status he sent to Rome; the others he punished himself—for their refusal to recant their religious identity, if not for any other infringement. Pliny's letter to Emperor Trajan for guidance is one of the first extra-

canonical pieces of evidence concerning Christian practice in this part of the Roman Empire.

Ep. 10.96: Pliny to Emperor Trajan

It is my custom, my lord, to refer to you everything about which I have any doubt. For who can better guide my hesitating steps or enlighten my ignorance? I have never been present at the trials of Christians. Furthermore, I do not know why they are usually investigated or punished or what the degree of punishment is. I am uncertain as to whether there ought to be consideration for age (are the very young to be treated differently from those who are more mature?); whether pardon is to be granted to those who repent; whether privilege is accorded an individual who was once a Christian but is one no longer; whether the name itself (if it is not blameless) or offenses associated with the name are to be punished.

Generally speaking, I have followed this procedure regarding those who are accused before me of being Christian: I have asked them whether they were Christians. If they confess, I question them a second and a third time, adding the threat of punishment. Without any hesitation, I sentence to punishment those who maintain their position. I have no doubt but that, whatever the nature of the crime they may have confessed, their stubbornness and inflexible obstinacy ought to be chastised. Others afflicted with a like madness have claimed to be Roman citizens; at my order, they were sent to Rome.

Then, in the course of the procedure, accusations increase and, as a result, several types of cases usually are presented. One anonymous accusation appeared before me, containing the names of many individuals. Some denied that they were or ever had been Christian. They called upon the gods, using the words I suggested. Some, with wine and incense, worshipped your image, which I had ordered to be brought in with the statues of the gods for this purpose, or they cursed Christ. (It is said that those who are actually Christian cannot be forced to do any of these things.) I thought these individuals ought to be acquitted. Others, named by an informer, said, at first, that they were Christian and then denied it, claiming that they had been so—some three years ago, others many years ago, one even twenty years before—but were no longer. All these persons worshipped your image and the statues of the gods, and cursed Christ.

However, they did maintain that the sum of their fault or error had been this: on an appointed day, before dawn, they were accustomed to meet together and to sing, in alternate choruses, a hymn to Christ as to a god; they bound themselves by oath not to commit any abomination, but to avoid theft, highway robbery, and adultery; not to betray any trust nor, when called on, to refuse to pay a deposit. Afterwards, it was their custom to depart and to reassemble later for a meal of ordinary, innocent food. They claimed that they had stopped this practice after I issued, at your order, an edict forbidding any gatherings. I believed it necessary to use torture in order to know the truth regarding two female servants, who were called deaconesses. I discovered nothing more than perverse and excessive superstition.

Thus, I have suspended my investigation so as to hasten to consult you. This matter, it seems to me, is worthy of consultation, especially because of the number of persons who are in danger. For there are many of all ages, all classes, and even of both sexes who are or will be summoned to justice. The infection of this superstition has penetrated not only cities, but villages and the countryside, as well. I believe it can be arrested and remedied.

In fact, the temples, which were almost completely abandoned, are once again being frequented; sacred festivals, long neglected, are being revived and fodder for sacrificial victims—for which, until recently, there were very few buyers—is again being sold. As a result, it is easy to imagine what a great number of people could be persuaded to amend their ways, if provision were made for their repentance.

Pliny's letter received a reply from the emperor. Trajan's letter reflects the first reported policy for imperial engagement with Christians.

Trajan to His Friend Pliny

In examining the cases of those who were brought before you accused as Christians, you have followed the procedure that you ought to have pursued, my friend Pliny. For, in such cases, it is impossible to establish a general rule which can be applied to each specific instance.

The Christians are not to be sought out. If they are accused and found guilty, they must be punished. However, if anyone of them denies being a Christian and clearly demonstrates this by offering prayers to our gods, that one is to be pardoned for the sake of repentance, whatever suspicion might have weighed on him in the past.

Furthermore, anonymous accusations are not to be taken into account, in any accusation at all. This is atrocious conduct and is unworthy of the age in which we live.

IV. Acts of the Martyrs of Scili

This martyr act describes the trial and sentence to death of a group of martyrs from Scili, a part of the African province of Numidia. The precise date of the text is unknown and may have been as late as the beginning of the third century; the events themselves, however, are depicted as having taken place at Carthage on July 17, 180 CE. *The text depicts an interrogation of the Christians by the proconsul and bears many of the hallmarks of the trial procedure already described in the Pliny/Trajan correspondence.*

When Praesens, for the second time, and Claudianus were the consuls, on the seventeenth day of July, at Carthage, there were placed in the judgment chamber Speratus, Nartzalus, Cittinus, Donata, Secunda, and Vestia.

Saturninus the proconsul said: "You can win the indulgence of our lord the Emperor, if you return to a sound mind."

Speratus said: "We have never done ill, we have not lent ourselves to any wrong, we have never spoken ill, but when ill-treated we have given thanks, because we pay heed to our Emperor." Saturninus the proconsul said: "We too are religious, and our religion is simple, and we swear by the genius of our lord the Emperor, and pray for his welfare, as you too ought to do."

Speratus said: "If you peaceably lend me your ears, I can tell you the mystery of simplicity."

Saturninus said: "I will not lend you my ears, when you begin to speak evil things of our sacred rites; but rather you swear by the genius of our lord the Emperor."

Speratus said: "I do not recognize the empire of this world; rather I serve that God whom no one has seen, nor can see with these eyes. I have committed no theft; but if I have bought anything I pay the tax; because I know my Lord, the King of kings and Emperor of all nations."

Saturninus the proconsul said to the others: "Cease to be of this persuasion."

Speratus said: "It is an evil persuasion to commit murder, to give false testimony."

Saturninus the proconsul said: "Do not be participants of this madness."

Cittinus said: "We do not have anyone else to fear, except only our Lord God, who is in heaven."

Donata said: "Honor to Caesar as Caesar—but fear to God."

Vestia said: "I am a Christian."

Secunda said: "I wish to be that which I am."

Saturninus the proconsul said to Speratus: "Do you persist in being a Christian?"

Speratus said: "I am a Christian." And with him they all agreed.

Saturninus the proconsul said: "Will you not have space to consider?"

Speratus said: "In such a reasonable matter there is no considering."

Saturninus the proconsul said: "What are the things in your box?"

Speratus said: "Books and epistles of Paul, a just man."

Saturninus the proconsul said: "Have a delay of thirty days and reconsider."

Speratus said a second time: "I am a Christian." And with him they all agreed.

Saturninus the proconsul read out the decree from the tablet: "Speratus, Nartzalus, Cittinus, Donata, Vestia, Secunda and the rest having confessed that they live according to the Christian rite, because after opportunity offered to them to return to the custom of the Romans they have obstinately persisted, it is determined that they be put to the sword."

Speratus said: "We give thanks to God."

Nartzalus said: "Today we are martyrs in heaven; thanks be to God."

Saturninus the proconsul ordered it to be declared by the herald: "I have ordered Speratus, Nartzalus, Cittinus, Veturius, Felix, Aquilinus, Laetantius, Januaria, Generosa, Vestia, Donata, and Secunda to be executed."

They all said: "Thanks be to God."

And so they all together were crowned with martyrdom; and they reign with the Father and the Son and the Holy Ghost for ever and ever. Amen.

V. Justin Martyr, The First Apology (c. 147–161 CE)

Justin, a self-styled Christian philosopher, here professes to address the Roman Emperor Antoninus Pius, his sons, and the entire senate on behalf of the Christians. The latter, Justin argues, have been unjustly persecuted; Justin does not deny that some who call themselves Christians might deserve punishment, but each case must be tried on its own merits if the leaders of the Roman Empire wish to show themselves just. In much of the Apology, *Justin expounds Christian doctrine and practice, highlighting the superior morality and civic-spiritedness of Christians; seeks to demonstrate Christ's provenance and identity from prophecy; and emphasizes the connections between Moses and the Greek philosopher Plato, even arguing that the latter's wisdom was dependent upon the former. The selections reproduced here deal with Justin's depiction of Christian morality and its compatibility with Roman laws and the needs of the empire.*

Chapter 1: Justin's Address

To Emperor Titus Aelius Adrianus Antoninus Pius Augustus Caesar; to his son Verissimus, the philosopher; to Lucius the philosopher, by birth son of Caesar and by adoption son of Pius, an admirer of learning; to the sacred Senate and to the whole Roman people; in behalf of those men of every race who are unjustly hated and mistreated: I, one of them, Justin, the son of Priscus and grandson of Bacchius, of the city of Flavia Neapolis in Syria-Palestine: do present this address and petition.

Chapter 2: Justin States His Objective: Fair Treatment of Christians

Common sense dictates that they who are truly pious men and philosophers should honor and cherish only what is true, and refuse to follow the beliefs of their forefathers, if these beliefs be worthless. For sound reason not only demands that we do not heed those who did or taught anything wrong, but it requires that the lover of truth must choose, in every way possible, to do and say what is right, even when threatened with death, rather than save his own life. You hear yourselves everywhere called pious men and philosophers, guardians of justice and lovers of learning: whether you really deserve this reputation will now become evident. Indeed, we have come not to flatter you with our writings or to curry your favor with this discourse, but to ask that, after an accurate and thorough examination, you hand down a decision that will not be influenced by prejudice or by the desire to please superstitious men; a decision that will not be the result of an irrational impulse or of an evil rumor long persistent, lest it become a judgment against yourselves. As far as we [Christians] are concerned, we believe that no evil can befall us unless we be convicted as criminals or be proved to be sinful persons. You, indeed, may be able to kill us, but you cannot harm us.

Chapter 10: Justin Explains the Superior Restraint of Divine vs. Human Laws

But we have learned from tradition that God has no need of the material gifts of men, since we see that He is the Giver of all things. We have been taught, are convinced, and do believe that He approves of only those who imitate His inherent virtues, namely, temperance, justice, love of man, and any other virtue proper to God who is called by no given name. We have also been instructed that God, in the beginning, created in His goodness everything out of shapeless matter for the sake of men. And if men by their actions prove themselves worthy of His plan, they shall, we are told, be found worthy to make their abode with Him and to reign with Him, free from all corruption and pain. Just as in the beginning He created us when we were not, so also, we believe, He will consider all those who choose to please Him, because of their choice, to be worthy of eternal life in His presence. Our creation was not in our own power. But this: to engage in those things that please Him and which we choose by means of the intellectual faculties He has bestowed on us—this makes our conviction and leads us to faith. Indeed, we think it is for the good of all men that they are not prevented from learning these things, but are even urged to consider them. For what human laws were unable to effect, the Divine Word would have accomplished, had not the evil demons enlisted the aid of the various utterly evil inclinations, which are in every man by nature, and scattered many false and ungodly accusations—none of which, however, applies to us.

Chapter 11: Justin Explains the Kingdom Christians Desire

When you hear that we look forward to a kingdom, you rashly assume that we speak of a human kingdom, whereas we mean a kingdom which is with God. This becomes evident when, being questioned, we openly profess to be Christians, although we know well that for such a profession of faith the punishment is death. If we expected a human kingdom, we would deny that we are Christians, that we might not be put to death, and we would try to hide from you, that we might attain what we expect. But because we do not place our hope in the present, we do not mind when men murder us, since death is inevitable anyhow.

Chapter 12: Justin Explains the Superior Watchfulness of God

We, more than all other men, are truly your helpers and allies in fostering peace, since we believe that it is impossible for the wicked, or the avaricious, or the treacherous, or the virtuous alike to hide from the sight of God, and that each man receives eternal punishment or salvation according to the merits of his actions. If everyone realized this, no one would prefer to be in sin even for a little while, knowing that he would incur the pains of eternal fire, but he would by all means control himself and adorn himself with virtue, in order to gain the favor of God and escape His punishments. It is not because of the laws and penalties you fix that men try to hide from you when they break the law, but they disobey the law knowing that it is possible to elude you, since you are mere men. If, however, they learned and were convinced that nothing, whether in their actions or in their thoughts, can be hidden from the knowledge of God, they would live a completely orderly life, if only because of the threatened punishments, as you yourselves will admit. But you seem to dread lest all men become just and you no longer have any left to punish. Such might be the worry of public executioners, but it should not be the concern of righteous rulers. As we said before, we believe that these things have been instigated by the evil demons who claim sacrifices and veneration even from those who do not live according to reason. But we do not presume that you who strive for piety and philosophy will act against reason. Still, if you, too, like thoughtless men, respect custom rather than truth, then do what is in your power. Rulers who prefer popular opinion to truth have as much power as robbers in the desert. That you will not succeed is testified to by the Word, and we know no ruler more kingly or just than He except God [the Father] who begot Him. For just as all men try to avoid inheriting the poverty, misery, and dishonor of their fathers, so will the man of reason refuse to choose whatever the Word forbids him to choose. That all these things should happen was foretold, I say, by our Teacher Jesus Christ, who is the Son and Apostle of God the Father and Ruler of all, and from whom we have received our name of Christians. Hence, we are convinced of the truth of all the things He taught us, because whatever He foretold would happen is actually happening; this, indeed, is the practice of God, to speak of something before it takes place and then to show it taking place just as He predicted. We might stop here and add nothing more, since we plead for what is just and true. But since we know how difficult it is to change over a mind trained in ignorance, we have decided to add a few observations to convince all lovers of truth, for we know that it is not impossible to dispel ignorance by setting truth against it.

Chapter 17: Justin Argues That Christ Himself Demands Civil Obedience from His Followers

As we have been instructed by Him, we, before all others, try everywhere to pay your appointed officials the ordinary and special taxes. For in His time some people came to Him and asked if it were necessary to pay tribute to Caesar, and He replied, "Tell Me, whose likeness does this coin bear?" They said, "Caesar's." And He again replied, "Render therefore to Caesar the things that are Caesar's, and to God, the things that are God's." Wherefore only God do we worship, but in other things we joyfully obey you, acknowledging you as the kings and rulers of men, and praying that you may be found to have, besides royal power, sound judgment. If you do not heed us, though we beseech you and clearly explain our position, it will by no means harm us, for we believe (rather, we are absolutely sure) that every man will pay the penalty of his misdeeds in the everlasting fire, and that everyone will give an account in proportion to the powers he received from God, as Christ made known to us when He said, "To whom God has given more, of him more shall be required."

Chapter 68: Justin Concludes His Remarks and Reiterates His Plea for Toleration

If you think our statements are in accordance with reason and truth, respect them; if they seem silly, despise them as such. But do not impose the death penalty against those who have done no wrong, as you would against your enemies. For we forewarn you that you shall not elude the future judgment of God, if you continue to be unjust; and we will exclaim, "Let God's will be done."

2

The Move toward the Center

VI. The "Edict of Milan" (313 CE)

As noted above, the so-called "Edict of Milan" was, technically speaking, neither an edict nor authored in Milan. As a Roman law, co-authored jointly by the Emperors Constantine and Licinius, it had the unprecedented effect of legalizing Christian worship and practice throughout the Roman Empire, as well as the restitution of Christian property that had been seized under the Diocletian persecution at the beginning of the fourth century.

For a long time now, recognizing that freedom of religion must not be denied but that each person must be assured the possibility of access to divine things according to his reason, his choice, and his preference, we have invited Christians to adhere to the faith of their sect and their religious belief. However, since many different conditions seem clearly to have been included in the edict in which this permission was granted to these very Christians, perhaps it has happened that some of them have been subsequently ostracized and hindered from practicing their religion.

When I, Constantine Augustus, and I, Licinius Augustus, met under happy auspices in Milan in order to discuss all the problems regarding security, the public welfare, and those matters which seemed to us to assure the good of the greater number, we believed it necessary to address, first of all, those matters which promote respect of the divine Being. In other words, we thought to grant to Christians, as to all people, the freedom and the possibility of following the religion of their choice. Thus, all that is divine in the heavenly abode might look with benevolence and kindness on us and on all who are subject to our authority. That is why, with salutary and just intention, we believed it necessary to decide never to refuse anyone the possibility of belonging to the Christian religion or to another which seemed better for that one. May the supreme divine Being, to whom we render free and enthusiastic homage, manifest his usual favor and goodness to us in all things. Thus it is right that Your Excellency know that we have decided to abolish the stipulations which seem to us entirely inopportune and foreign to our mercy. We suppress completely the restrictions concerning Christians, contained in documents sent to you previously. Henceforth, we grant to all those who are determined to follow the Christian religion the right to do so freely and without reservation. They are not to be harassed or molested.

We have thought it necessary to bring these decisions in their fullness to Your Concern, in order that you may know well that we have granted to these Christians open and entire permission to practice their religion.

Realizing fully that we grant them this right, Your

Devotedness knows that the same possibility of practicing religion and cult openly and freely is assured to all other citizens, as is appropriate to our era of peace, so that every individual might have the liberty of participating in the worship of his choice. Our decision has been motivated by the desire to avoid even the appearance of having placed the least restriction on any cult or on any religion.

Furthermore, this is what we have deemed it necessary to decide, concerning the community of Christians: the places treated under particular instructions in the letters sent previously to you—places where Christians formerly customarily assembled—are to be restored to them without cost or any other required indemnity. All trickery or ambiguous behavior in this matter is out of the question on the part of those who are supposed to have purchased these properties earlier, either through our treasury or through any other agent. In the same manner, those who have acquired these places gratuitously must also return them to the Christians as soon as possible. Furthermore, if those who have acquired these possessions through purchase or donation claim any compensation from our kindness, they are to present themselves to our representative so that, through our indulgence, their concerns also may be addressed.

All these places are to be returned to the community of the Christians through your representative, immediately and without delay. It is a fact that the Christians possessed not only the places where they ordinarily assembled, but other property as well. These properties belonged by right to their communities—that is, to churches and not to individuals. You are to restore to these Christians—that is, to their community and to their church—all such property, on the conditions mentioned above, without any question or dispute whatsoever.

The one exception, already referred to, is that those who restore any property received gratuitously can expect to be reimbursed through our graciousness. In all of this, you are to give your most efficacious support to the community of Christians to which we have referred, so that our mandate might be fulfilled as soon as possible, and also that, in this way, our concern for public tranquillity might be fostered. It is only thus, as we have noted above, that the divine favor which we have experienced in the most serious situations in the past will continue to assure the success of our undertakings, for such is the pledge of public prosperity.

Moreover, so that the application of our generous prescription may be brought to the knowledge of all, it is fitting that these decisions be promulgated by you in proclamation, in notices posted everywhere, and that you bring this news to the attention of all the people. In this way, no one can remain ignorant of the decision made by us in a spirit of benevolence.

VII. Eusebius Pamphilius, *The Life of Constantine* (c. 339 CE)

Eusebius's Life of Constantine *should be read as much as a panegyric, a speech of exuberant praise, as it should be treated as narrative history or biography as modern readers conceive of it. Constantine had died in 337 CE, and the concluding portions of the book address his legacy; however, Eusebius himself died two years later, leaving the work either unfinished or perhaps unrevised. Here as elsewhere, Eusebius does not hesitate to portray him as a paragon of Christian virtue, a champion of the churches, an arbiter of ecclesiastical peace, and in many ways a source of divine blessing for the Christians of the empire who had just decades earlier suffered under Diocletian's persecution. Excerpted here are a selection of the best-known chapters that address Constantine's religious experience and policy.*

Constantine Prepares for Battle against Maxentius and Decides to Call on God

1.27: [1] Knowing well that he would need more powerful aid than an army can supply because of the mischievous magical devices practiced by the tyrant, he sought a god to aid him. He regarded the resources of soldiers and military numbers as secondary, for he thought that without the aid of a god these could achieve nothing; and he said that what comes from a god's assistance is irresistible and invincible. [2] He therefore considered what kind of god he should adopt to aid him, and while he thought, a clear impression came to him that of the many who had in the past aspired to government, those who had attached their personal hopes to many gods and had cultivated them with drink-offerings, sacrifices, and dedications had first been deceived by favorable predictions and oracles which promised welcome things, but then met an unwelcome end, nor did any god stand at their side to protect them from divinely directed disaster; only his own father had taken the opposite course to theirs by condemning their error, while he himself had throughout his life honored the God who transcends the universe, and had found him a savior and guardian of his empire and a provider of everything good. [3] He judiciously considered these things for himself, and weighed well how those who had confided in a multitude of gods had run into multiple destruction, so that neither spring nor shoot was left in them, no root, neither name nor memorial among mankind, whereas his father's God had bestowed on his father manifest and numerous tokens of his power. He also pondered carefully those who had already campaigned against the tyrant. They had assembled their forces with a multitude of gods and had come to a dismal end: one of them had retreated in disgrace without striking a blow, while the other had met a casual death by assassination in his own camp. He marshalled these arguments in his mind and concluded that it was folly to go on with the vanity of the gods which do not exist, and to persist in error in the face of so much evidence; and he decided he should venerate his father's God alone.

Constantine's Vision

1.28: [1] This God he began to invoke in prayer, beseeching and imploring him to show him who he was, and to stretch out his right hand to assist him in his plans. As he made these prayers and earnest supplications there appeared to the emperor a most remarkable divine sign. If someone else had reported it, it would perhaps not be easy to accept; but since the victorious emperor himself told the story to the present writer a long while after, when I was privileged with his acquaintance and company, and confirmed it with oaths, who could hesitate to believe the account, especially when the time which followed provided evidence for the truth of what he said? [2] About the time of the midday sun, when day was just turning, he said he saw with his own eyes, up in the sky and resting over the sun, a cross-shaped trophy formed from light, and a text attached to it which said, "By this conquer." Amazement at the spectacle seized both him and the whole company of soldiers which was then accompanying him on a campaign he was conducting somewhere, and witnessed the miracle.

1.29–30: He was, he said, wondering to himself what the

manifestation might mean; then, while he meditated and thought long and hard, night overtook him. Thereupon, as he slept, the Christ of God appeared to him with the sign which had appeared in the sky, and urged him to make himself a copy of the sign which had appeared in the sky, and to use this as protection against the attacks of the enemy. When day came he arose and recounted the mysterious communication to his friends. Then he summoned goldsmiths and jewellers, sat down among them, and explained the shape of the sign, and gave them instructions about copying it in gold and precious stones. . . .

32.1: . . . At the time in question, stunned by the amazing vision and determined to worship no other god than the one who had appeared, he summoned those expert in his words and enquired who this god was, and what was the explanation of the vision which had appeared of the sign. [2] They said that the god was the only begotten Son of the one and only God, and that the sign which appeared was a token of immortality, and was an abiding trophy of the victory over death, which he had once won when he was present on earth. They began to teach him the reasons for his coming, explaining to him in detail the story of his self-accommodation to human conditions. [3] He listened attentively to these accounts too, while he marvelled at the divine manifestation which had been granted to his eyes; comparing the heavenly vision with the meaning of what was being said, he made up his mind, convinced that it was as God's own teaching that the knowledge of these things had come to him. He now decided personally to apply himself to the divinely inspired writings. Taking the priests of God as his advisers, he also deemed it right to honor the God who had appeared to him with all due rites. Thereafter, fortified by good hopes in him, he finally set about extinguishing the menacing flames of tyranny.

After his victory and establishment as emperor, Constantine takes charge of matters of Christian policy, including convening the Council of Nicea to settle contentions concerning the nature of Christ and the date of Easter.

Constantine Addresses the Assembled Bishops

3.11: The bishop who was first in the row on the right then stood up and delivered a rhythmical speech, addressing the emperor, and offering a hymn of gratitude for him to God the Ruler of all. When he too had sat down, silence fell on all as they gazed intently at the emperor. He with shining eyes looked kindly on them all, and then, collecting his thoughts, in a soft and gentle voice he gave a speech somewhat like this:

3.12: [1] "It was the object of my prayers, my friends, to share in your company, and now that I have received this, I know I must express my gratitude to the King of all, because in addition to everything else He has allowed me to see this, which is better than any other good thing; I mean, to receive you all gathered together and to observe one unanimous opinion shared by all. [2] Let no jealous enemy ruin our prosperity; now that the war of the tyrants against God has been swept away by the power of God the Savior, let not the malignant demon encompass the divine law with blasphemies by other means. For to me internal division in the church of God is graver than any war or fierce battle, and these things appear to cause more pain than secular airs. [3] When therefore I won victories over enemies through the favor and support of the Supreme, I considered that nothing remained but to give thanks to God, and to rejoice also with those who had been liberated by him through our agency. When contrary to all expectation I learned of your division, I did not defer attention to the report, but, praying that this too might be healed through my ministration, I immediately sent for you all. [4] I rejoice to see your gathering, and I consider that I shall be acting most in accordance with my prayers, when I see you all with your souls in communion, and one common, peaceful harmony prevailing among you all, which you, as persons consecrated to God, ought yourselves to be announcing to others. [5] So do not delay, my friends, ministers of God, and good servants of the common Lord and Savior of us all, to begin now to bring the causes of the division between you into the open, and to loosen all shackles of dispute by the laws of peace. Thus you will both achieve what is pleasing to the God of all, and you will give extreme gratification to me, your fellow servant."

Eusebius also depicts Constantine as the sponsor of great Christian building projects, none more impressive than the Anastasis, the Church of the Holy Sepulchre in Jerusalem.

Constantine Commissions the Anastasis

3.29: [1] With [the excavation of the Holy Sepulchre] thus completed, the emperor next gave orders by the stipulations of pious laws and by generous grants for a place of worship worthy of God to be built with rich and imperial munificence around the Savior's cave, as if he had intended this for a long time and had looked into the future with superior foreknowledge. [2] He instructed those who governed the eastern provinces by generous and lavish grants to make the building out of the ordinary, huge, and rich, and to the bishop of the church who then presided in Jerusalem, he sent the following document. By it he displayed in clear terms the love for God in his own soul and the purity of his faith in the Savior's Word, writing in this fashion:

3.30: [1] Victor Constantinus Maximus Augustus to Macarius.

So great is our Savior's grace that no words seem enough to match the present miracle. For the evidence of His most sacred passion, long since hidden under the ground, to have remained unknown for such a long period of years, until through the removal of the enemy of the whole republic it was ready to be revealed, once they were set free, to his servants, truly surpasses all marvels. [2] If all those from every part of the world with a reputation for wisdom were to gather together in one place and try to say something worthy of the event, they would not be able to compete with the least part of it. The evidence of this miracle surpasses every natural capacity of human thought in the same degree that heavenly things are by common consent mightier than human. [3] That is why it is always my first and only goal that, just as the evidence for the truth manifests itself with newer wonders every day, so all our souls may by utter seriousness and unanimous endeavor also become more earnest about the holy law. [4] The thing therefore which I consider clear to everybody is what I want you in particular to believe, namely that above all else my concern is that that sacred place, which at God's command I have now relieved of the hideous burden of an idol which lay on it like a weight, hallowed from the start by God's decree, and now proved yet holier since it brought to light the pledge of the Savior's passion, should be adorned by us with beautiful buildings.

3.31: [1] It is thus for your own Good Sense to make such order and provision of what is needed, that not only a basilica superior to those in all other places, but the other arrangements also, may be such that all the excellences of every city are surpassed by this foundation. [2] As to the building and decoration of the walls, be advised that our friend Dracillianus, who exercises his office among the *praefecti illustrissimi*, and he who is governor of the province have been entrusted by us with its care. For my Religious Care has ordered that craftsmen and labourers and everything they may learn from your Good Sense to be needed for the building work should forthwith be supplied by their provision. [3] As to the columns of marble, you should after a survey yourself write promptly to us about what you may consider to be of most value and use, so that whatever quantity and kind of materials we may learn from your letter to be needful may be competently supplied from all sources. It is right that the world's most miraculous place should be worthily embellished. 3.32: [1] As to the vault of the basilica, whether you decide that it be coffered or in another style of construction I would wish to learn from you. If it were to be coffered, it might also be decorated with gold. [2] In short, in order that your Holiness may make known with all speed to the aforementioned magistrates how many labourers and craftsmen and what other expenditures are required, take care to refer immediately also to me not only the matters of the marble and pillars, but also the lacunary panels, should you judge that best.

God preserve you, dear Brother.

3.33: [1] Thus did the emperor write. No sooner had he written than the commands were put into effect. New Jerusalem was built at the very Testimony to the Savior, facing the famous Jerusalem of old, which after the bloody murder of the Lord had been overthrown in utter devastation, and paid the penalty of its wicked inhabitants. [2] Opposite this then the emperor erected the victory of the Savior over death with rich and abundant munificence, this being perhaps that fresh new Jerusalem proclaimed in prophetic oracles, about which long speeches recite innumerable praises as they utter words of divine inspiration.

Eusebius describes at great length Constantine's personal piety. His baptism, however, the emperor delayed until his health was failing and he was very nearly on his deathbed.

Constantine's Baptism

4.61: [1] First a bodily indisposition came upon him, then illness supervened, and thereupon he went out to the hot water baths of his city, and from there to the city named after his mother.

There he spent his time at the chapel of the martyrs, and offered up supplicatory prayers and petitions to God. [2] But when he became aware that his life was ending, he perceived that this was the time to purify himself from the offenses which he had at any time committed, trusting that, whatever sins it had been his lot as mortal to commit, he could wash them from his soul by the power of the secret words and the saving bath. [3] Having perceived this, he knelt on the floor and made himself a suppliant to God, making confession in the martyrion itself, where also he was first accorded the prayers that go with laying on of hands. He left there and reached as far as the suburbs of Nicomedia. There he called together the bishops and addressed them thus: 4.62: [1] "This is the moment I have long hoped for, as I thirsted and yearned to win salvation in God. It is our time too to enjoy the seal that brings immortality, time to enjoy the sealing that gives salvation, [2] which I once intended to receive at the streams of the river Jordan, where our Savior also is reported to have received the bath as an example to us. But God who knows what is good for us judges us worthy of these things here and now. [3] So let there be no delay. If the Lord of life and death should wish us to live again here, even so it is once and for all decided that I am hereafter numbered among the people of God, and that I meet and join in the prayers with them all together. I shall now set for myself rules of life which befit God."

[4] Such were his words. They in their turn, performing the customary rites, fulfilled the divine laws and imparted the secret gifts, giving such preliminary instruction as is required. Alone of all the emperors from the beginning of time Constantine was initiated by rebirth in the mysteries of Christ, and exulted in the Spirit on being vouchsafed the divine seal, and was renewed and filled with divine light, rejoicing in his

soul because of his intense faith, awestruck at the manifestation of the divinely inspired power.

[5] When the due ceremonies were complete, he put on bright imperial clothes which shone like light, and rested on a pure white couch, being unwilling to touch a purple robe again. 4.63: [1] Then he lifted up his voice and offered up a prayer of thanksgiving to God, after which he went on to say, "I know that now I am in the true sense blessed, that now I have been shown worthy of immortal life, that now I have received divine light." He went on to call those persons wretched, and said they were pitiable, who did not share those good things. [2] When the tribunes and senior officers from the armies filed in and lamented, bewailing their own imminent bereavement, and wished him extension of life, he answered them too by saying that he enjoyed true life now, and only he knew the good things he had received; they were therefore to hasten his journey to God and not postpone it. [3] Thereupon he made disposition of his property. The Romans who lived in the imperial city he honored with annual grants. On his sons he bestowed as a father's estate the inheritance of empire, having arranged everything as he desired.

4.64: [1] Each of these events took place during the greatest festival, the utterly sacred and holy Pentecost, honored with seven weeks and sealed up with a single day, during which divine words describe the ascension into Heaven of the universal Savior and the descent of the Holy Spirit upon mankind. [2] Being granted these things during the festival, on the last day of all, which one might not inaccurately call the Feast of feasts, about the time of the midday sun the emperor was taken up to his God; he bequeathed to mortals what was akin to them, but he himself, with that part of him which is the soul's intelligence and love of God, was united to his God. That was the end of the life of Constantine.

Eusebius concludes his remarks by reiterating Constantine's uniqueness among Roman rulers.

4.74–75: Having shown these things to our very eyes in the case of Constantine alone in all time, who was transparently displayed as a Christian, God who is over all exhibited how great was the difference for him between those who have seen fit to worship him and his Christ and those who choose the opposite. They, by setting out to attack His church, made him their own enemy and adversary, and the disastrous end of the life of each one indicated the manifest punishment for their hostility to God, just as the end of Constantine made plain to everybody the rewards of the love of God. He alone of all the Roman emperors has honored God the All-sovereign with exceeding godly piety; he alone has publicly proclaimed to all the word of Christ; he alone has honored His church as no other since time began; he alone has destroyed all polytheistic error, and exposed every kind of idolatry; and surely he alone has deserved in life itself and after death such things as none could say has ever been achieved by any other among either Greeks or barbarians, or even among the ancient Romans, for his like has never been recorded from the beginning of time until our day.

VIII. Ephrem, Third Hymn against Julian (c. 363 CE)

Unlike many of our other sources, Ephrem's takes the form a hymn, to be chanted rather than simply read. As such, it has many of the hallmarks of that more poetic genre. Ephrem here retells the arrival of the corpse of the Roman emperor Julian, who had abandoned

Christianity in favor of a return to the worship of the Roman gods, at Nisibis, where the Roman army had been badly beaten by its Sassanid opponents. The city was lost to the Sassanids, and a peace-accord between the two empires was negotiated by Julian's successor, Jovian, a Christian. Ephrem, who witnessed the battle and its aftermath, depicts the events as God's punishment of Julian.

A wonder!
By chance the corpse of that accursed one,
crossing over toward the rampart, met me near the city!
And the Magus took and fastened on a tower
the standard sent from the east,[1]
so that this standard-bearer would declare to the onlookers
that the city was slave to the lords of that standard.

Refrain: Glory to the One Who wrapped the corpse in shame!

I wondered, "Who indeed set a time for meeting
when corpse[2] and standard-bearer both at one moment were present?"
I knew it was a prearrangement, a miracle of justice
that when the corpse of the fallen one crossed over,
the fearful standard went up and was put in place to proclaim
that the evil of his conjurers had surrendered that city.
For thirty years Persia had made battle in every way
but was unable to cross over the boundary of that city;
even when it had been broken and collapsed, the cross came down and saved it.
There I saw a disgraceful sight:

1. The standard in question would indicate to onlookers that the city of Nisibis was now under the control of the Sassanids, having been lost to the Roman Empire as divine punishment for Julian's abandonment of the Christian faith, Ephrem argues.
2. Ephrem here refers to the corpse of the apostate emperor, Julian.

the standard of the captor set up on the tower,
the corpse of the persecutor laid in a coffin.
Believe in "yes" and "no," the word of a trustworthy man,
that I went right up, my brothers, to the coffin of the filthy one,
and I stood over him and derided his paganism
and said, "Is this indeed he who exalted himself
against the Living Name and forgot that he is dust?"
[God] turned him back into his dust to let him know he was of dust.
I stood and wondered at him whose downfall I had so fully seen.
"This is his majesty and this is his pomp!
This is his kingship and this is his chariot!
This is a clump of earth that has disintegrated!"
I argued with myself, "Why in [the time of] his power
did I not foresee this would be his end?"
I wondered about the many who, in seeking to please
the diadem of mortality, denied the universal Life-giver.
I looked above and below and was amazed, my brothers,
at our Lord [in] His height, the Glorious One,
and the accursed one in [his] downfall, and I said, "Who will fear
this corpse and deny the True One?"
He prevented the cross that came down from gaining victory,
not because the victorious [cross] was unable to gain victory,
but so that a pit might be dug for the evildoer
who came down with his conjurers to the east.
But since he came down and was struck, the discerning saw
that the battle in which he would be put to shame had been lying in wait for him.
Know that because of this the time was long and delayed
so that the pure one might complete the years of his kingship

and the accursed one might also complete the measure of his paganism.[3]
But when he had completed his story, he came to ruin.
So both sides rejoiced, and so there was peace
through the believing king, companion of the glorious [kings].[4]
The Just One by all [manner] of deaths was capable of destroying him,
but he kept [for him] a downfall fearful and bitter,
so that on the day of his death all things should be drawn up before his eyes:
Where is that oracle that reassured him?
and the goddess of weapons, that she did not come to his aid?
and the companies of his gods, that they did not come to save him?
The cross of the All-knowing marched before the army.
It endured being mocked: "It cannot save them!"[5]
It kept the king in safety; it gave the army to destruction,
for it knew that paganism [was] among them.[6]
Let the cross of Him Who searches all, therefore, be praised—
[the cross] that fools without discernment reviled at that time.
For they did not persevere with the standard of the Savior of all.
Indeed that paganism that they showed in the end
was manifest to our Lord from the beginning.
Yet although He knew well that they were pagans,

3. Constantius, Julian's Christian predecessor, needed to complete his reign, and Julian needed to bring his own paganism to its full measure before God would in such a way intervene, Ephrem suggests.
4. Both Romans and Sassanids, Ephrem reports, rejoiced over the peace treaty negotiated by Jovian, Julian's Christian successor, even though Nisibis under this treaty fell to the Sassanids.
5. Despite Julian's rejection of Christianity, the cross was among the standards carried by the Roman army at Nisibis.
6. The king in question here is certainly not Julian, who died in battle, but perhaps the preceding emperor, Constantius.

His cross saved them, but when they apostatized from Him,
they ate corpses there; they became a parable there.[7]
When the People was defeated at Ai of the weak,
Joshua tore his garments before the Ark [of the Covenant]
and spoke fearful [words] before the Most High.
A curse [was] among the People, without his knowing.[8]
Just so paganism was hidden in the army,
but instead of the Ark they were carrying the cross.
But Justice summoned him with wisdom,
for not by force did she govern his freedom.
By an enticement he marched out to the lance that struck:
he saw that he subdued citadels, and he became proud.
For adversity did not cry out to him to turn back
until he marched out and fell into the midst of the vortex.
The lance of Justice passed through the belly of him
who despised Him Who made the lance of paradise pass away.
The divination of the conjurers tore open a pregnant [animal].[9]
[Julian] groaned at length to recall
what he had written and published that he would do to the churches.
The finger of Justice blotted out his memory.
The king saw that easterners came and deceived him.
Simple men [deceived] the wise man; common men [deceived] the diviner.
Those whom he, wrapped up in his vestment,[10] summoned,
confined his wisdom by ignorant men,
and he gave orders to set fire to his victorious ships,

7. Julian's army at Nisibis was apparently in sufficiently dire straits to resort to cannibalism; their desperation became proverbial, Ephrem suggests.
8. Josh. 7:1-26.
9. Ephrem here refers to the practice of divination by reading the innards of an animal to discern the future.
10. Ephrem here refers to Julian's, like other Roman emperors', wearing the priestly garment of Pontifex Maximus.

and his idols and diviners were entangled in a trap.
But when he saw that his gods were confuted and exposed
and that he could neither gain victory nor flee,
[that] between fear and disgrace he was prostrate and beaten,
he chose death to escape into Sheol.
Cunningly he stripped off his armor in order to be wounded,
in order to die so that the Galileans would not see his shame.[11]
For he had mockingly named the brothers Galileans.[12]
Behold in the air the wheels of the Galilean King![13]
He thunders in His chariot; the cherubim bear Him.
The Galilean revealed [the chariot] and handed over
the flock of the soothsayer to the wolves in the wilderness,
but the Galilean herd increased and filled the whole earth.

11. Ephrem here refers to the suggestion, corroborated by other historians, that Julian's corpse was found without his armor.
12. Ephrem here refers to Julian's well-known—if no longer preserved—anti-Christian treatise *Against the Galileans.*
13. Ephrem here refers to the heavenly chariot bearing Christ.

3

Christians at the Heart of the Empire

IX. The Theodosian Code (438 CE)

Commissioned by the Emperor Theodosius II in 429 CE and published nine years later, the Theodosian Code reflects an effort, unprecedented in Roman legal history, to gather the numerous laws that had been handed down by Christian emperors since 312 CE into one comprehensive collection. The sixteen books of the Theodosian Code contain more than 2,500 such laws, with each book dedicated to a particular topic. The selections reproduced here come from Book 16, dedicated to matters of religion; they are merely a small excerpt of the material contained therein, but are designed to give readers a glimpse into Roman law-making as it pertains to Christians and other religious groups.

16.2.4: Emperors Gratian, Valentinian, and Theodosius Augustuses: An Edict to the People of the City of Constantinople

The famous "Cunctos Populos" edict, ordering all citizens of the Roman Empire to share the faith of the bishops of Rome and Alexandria, and making pro-Nicene Christianity the official religion of the Roman Empire.

It is Our will that all the peoples who are ruled by the administration of Our Clemency shall practice that religion which the divine Peter the Apostle transmitted to the Romans, as the religion which he introduced makes clear even unto this day. It is evident that this is the religion that is followed by the Pontiff Damasus and by Peter, Bishop of Alexandria, a man of apostolic sanctity; that is, according to the apostolic discipline and the evangelic doctrine, we shall believe in the single Deity of the Father, the Son, and the Holy Spirit, under the concept of equal majesty and of the Holy Trinity.

We command that those persons who follow this rule shall embrace the name of Catholic Christians. The rest, however, whom We adjudge demented and insane, shall sustain the infamy of heretical dogmas, their meeting places shall not receive the name of churches, and they shall be smitten first by divine vengeance and secondly by the retribution of Our own initiative, which We shall assume in accordance with the divine judgment.

Given on the third day before the kalends of March at Thessaloniki in the year of the fifth consulship of Gratian Augustus and the first consulship of Theodosius Augustus (February 28, 380).

16.2.41. The Same Augustuses[1] to Melitius, Praetorian Prefect

An edict requiring Christian clergy to face legal charges only before a bishop, who would function as an arbiter, rather than before a magistrate or another civic authority.

Clerics must not be accused except before bishops. Therefore, if a bishop, a priest, a deacon, or any person of inferior rank who is a minister of the Christian faith should be accused by any person whatever before the bishops, since he must not be accused elsewhere, that man, whether of lofty honor or of any other dignity, who may undertake such a laudable type of suit, shall know that he must allege only what may be demonstrated by proofs and supported by documents. If any man, therefore, should lodge unprovable complaints about such persons, he shall understand that by the authority of this sanction he will be subject to the loss of his own reputation, and thus by the loss of his honor and the forfeiture of his status he shall learn that he will not be permitted, for the future at least, to assail with impunity the respect due to another. For, just as it is equitable that bishops, priests, deacons, and all other clerics should be removed from the venerable church as persons attainted if the allegations against them can be proved, so that they shall be despised thereafter and bowed under the contempt of wretched humiliation and shall not have an action for slander, so it must appear to be an act of similar justice that We have ordered an appropriate punishment for assailed innocence. Bishops, therefore, must hear such cases only under the attestation of many persons and in formal proceedings.

Given on the third day before the ides of December at

1. Namely, Emperors Arcadius and Honorius.

Ravenna in the year of the ninth consulship of Honorius Augustus and the fifth consulship of Theodosius Augustus (December 12, 412; 411).

16.5.38. The Same Augustuses[2] and Theodosius Augustus: An Edict

An edict outlawing Manicheism and Donatism.

No one shall recall to memory a Manichean, no one a Donatist, who especially, as We have learned, do not cease their madness. There shall be one Catholic worship, one salvation; equal sanctity within the Trinity, harmonious within itself, shall be sought. But if any person should dare to participate in practices that are interdicted and unlawful, he shall not escape the toils of innumerable previous constitutions and of the law that was recently issued by Our Clemency. If perchance seditious mobs should assemble, he shall not doubt that the sharp goads of a more severe punishment will be applied to him.

Given on the day before the ides of February at Ravenna in the year of the second consulship of Stilicho and the consulship of Anthemius (February 12, 405).

16.5.41. The Same Augustuses[3] to Porphyrius, Proconsul of Africa

A law establishing repentance and conversion to the Nicene faith as a full defense against charges of Donatism, Manicheism, or other forms of heresy.

2. Namely, Emperors Arcadius and Honorius.
3. Once more, Emperors Arcadius and Honorius.

Although it is customary for crimes to be expiated by punishment, it is Our will, nevertheless, to correct the depraved desires of men by an admonition to repentance. Therefore, if any heretics, whether they are Donatists or Manicheans or of any other depraved belief and sect who have congregated for profane rites, should embrace, by a simple confession, the Catholic faith and rites, which We wish to be observed by all men, even though such heretics have nourished a deep-rooted evil by long and continued meditation, to such an extent that they also seem to be subject to the laws formerly issued, nevertheless, as soon as they have confessed God by a simple expression of belief, We decree that they shall be absolved from all guilt. Thus for every criminal offense, whether it was committed before or should be committed afterward, a thing which We regret, although punishment seems to be especially urgent for the guilty, it shall suffice for annulment that they should condemn their false doctrine by their own judgment and should embrace the name of almighty God, which they may call upon even in the midst of their perils; for when the succor of religion has been invoked, it must nowhere be absent in afflictions. Therefore, just as We order that the previous laws which We have issued for the destruction of sacrilegious minds shall be forcefully pressed to the full effect of their execution, in like manner We decree that those persons who have preferred the faith of pure religion, even though by late confession, shall not be bound by the laws which have been issued. We sanction the foregoing regulations in order that all persons may know that the infliction of punishment on the profane desires of men shall not be lacking, and that it redounds to the advantage of true worship that the support of the laws should also be present.

Given on the seventeenth day before the kalends of December at Rome in the year of the seventh consulship of Honorius Augustus and the second consulship of Theodosius Augustus (November 15, 407).

16.6.2. Emperors Valens, Gratian, and Valentinian Augustuses to Florianus, Vicar of Asia

A law regulating Christian practice by outlawing re-baptism, a practice common particularly among Donatist Christians but rejected by the church catholic.

We condemn the false doctrine of those persons who trample under foot the precepts of the Apostles and who do not purify, but defile by a second baptism, those persons who have received the sacraments of the Christian name, and thus pollute them in the name of the baptismal font. Your Authority shall therefore order them to desist from their miserable false doctrines, and the churches which they retain contrary to good faith shall be restored to the Catholic Church. The teachings, indeed, of those persons who have approved the Apostolic faith without any change of baptism shall be followed. For it is Our will that nothing shall be taught except what the uncorrupted faith and tradition of the Evangelists and Apostles have preserved, just as the imperial law of Our Fathers, Constantine, Constantius, and Valentinian, have decreed.

But very many persons who have been expelled from the churches go about, nevertheless, with secret madness, frequenting unlawfully the places of great houses or estates. Such estates shall be included in the fiscal confiscation if they should provide secret places for the sinful doctrine. Moreover, Our sanction shall not derogate any thing from the law which was previously established in a regulation that was given to

Nitentius. But if they love their false doctrine, they shall cherish the poison of their impious doctrine to their own hurt, in domestic secrecy and alone.

Given on the sixteenth day before the kalends of November at Constantinople in the year of the fourth consulship of Gratian Augustus and the consulship of Merobaudes (October 17, 377).

16.7.1. Emperors Gratian, Valentinian, and Theodosius Augustuses to Eutropius, Praetorian Prefect

A law preventing Christians who convert to paganism from making a will.

Those Christians who have become pagans shall be deprived of the power and right to make testaments, and every testament of such decedent, if there is a testament, shall be rescinded by the annulment of its foundation.

Given on the sixth day before the nones of May at Constantinople in the year of the consulship of Syagrius and Eucherius (May 2, 381).

16.8.7. The Same Augustus[4] and Julian Caesar to Thalassius, Praetorian Prefect

A law stripping Christians who convert to Judaism of all their property.

In accordance with the venerable law which has been established, We command that if any person should be converted from Christianity to Judaism and should join their

4. Namely, Emperor Constantius.

sacrilegious gatherings, when the accusation has been proved, his property shall be vindicated to the ownership of the fisc.

Given on the fifth day before the nones of July at Milan in the year of the ninth consulship of Constantius Augustus and the second consulship of Julian Caesar (July 3, 357; 352; 353).

16.10.4. The Same Augustuses[5] to Taurus, Praetorian Prefect

A law requiring the closing of all pagan temples.

It is Our pleasure that the temples shall be immediately closed in all places and in all cities, and access to them forbidden, so as to deny to all abandoned men the opportunity to commit sin. It is also Our will that all men shall abstain from sacrifices. But if perchance any man should perpetrate any such criminality, he shall be struck down with the avenging sword. We also decree that the property of a man thus executed shall be vindicated to the fisc. The governors of the provinces shall be similarly punished if they should neglect to avenge such crimes.

Given on the kalends of December in the year of the fourth consulship of Constantius Augustus and the third consulship of Constans Augustus (December 1, 346; 354; 356).

16.10.17. The Same Augustuses[6] to Apollodorus, Proconsul of Africa

A law nevertheless preserving pagan festivals as legal practice.

Just as We have already abolished profane rites by a salutary law, so We do not allow the festal assemblies of citizens and the

5. Namely, Emperors Constantius and Constans.
6. Namely, Emperors Arcadius and Honorius.

common pleasure of all to be abolished. Hence We decree that, according to ancient custom, amusements shall be furnished to the people, but without any sacrifice or any accursed superstition, and they shall be allowed to attend festal banquets, whenever public desires so demand.

Given on the thirteenth day before the kalends of September at Padua in the year of the consulship of the Most Noble Theodorus (August 20, 399).

X. Libanius's Oration 30: *For the Temples* (c. 384 CE)

Libanius was a sophist, a rhetor, and teacher of rhetoric in Antioch in the fourth century. The art of rhetoric, while today largely lost, was one of the essentials of higher education in the Roman Empire. It prepared students to embark on careers in the Roman courts, in law and civil service. Christians, too, pursued such an education, and among Libanius's best-known pupils are such patristic greats as Basil of Caesarea and John Chrysostom. Libanius himself, however, followed the old pagan gods, and evidently regarded aspects of the new religion, Christianity, with dismay.

Oration 30 is an appeal to the Christian Emperor Theodosius to protect the temples from the violence of Christian monks who had endeavored to destroy them as potential obstacles to new converts. Libanius regarded such "self-help" as reprehensible, and his oration leaves little doubt just how poorly he thought of at least some of his Christian contemporaries. The following excerpt nevertheless allows readers a glimpse into the challenges of Christianization of an empire—the difficulties of evangelizing a rural population, and the anxieties of the empire's elites.

1. On many previous occasions, Sire, when I have tendered advice, you have felt that I have reached a proper conclusion, and I have prevailed over those whose words and wishes were

opposed to mine because of the superior merits of my counsel. Now too I come on the same errand, inspired with the same hope, and now too especially lend me your ears. If, however, I fail to convince you, do not consider the speaker to be hostile to your administration. Apart from anything else, reflect upon the great distinction you have bestowed upon me and consider that the beneficiary cannot but reasonably feel the strongest affection for his benefactor. Simply for this reason I feel that I must advise on matters where I believe I have something worthwhile to say. In no other way could I show my gratitude to my sovereign, only perhaps by my oratory and what follows from it.

2. To many people it will appear that I am courting much danger by embarking upon an address to you about the temples and the need for them not to be abused as they are now, but in my view such people, in entertaining these fears, are very much mistaken in their assessment of you. To my mind, it is the choleric, ill-tempered man who proceeds immediately to condemn the expression of opinions, when anything is said that is displeasing to him: the kindly, humane, gentle character—your own qualities, Sire—merely refuses the counsel of which he does not approve. For where it lies with the hearer of a discourse whether to be convinced by it or not, it is unjustified for him to refuse a hearing, since no harm can come of it, or to become angry and resort to punishment if he disagrees with any remarks when anyone has the courage to say what he conceives to be right.

4. The first men who appeared on earth, Sire, occupied the high places and protected themselves in caves and huts, and soon gained a notion of gods and realized how much their good

will means to mankind. They raised the kind of temples to be expected of primitive man and made idols for themselves. As their culture advanced towards urbanization and building techniques became adequate for it, many cities made their appearance at the mountain's foot or on the plains, and in each and every one of them the first buildings to be erected after the wall were shrines and temples, for they believed that from such governance they would have the utmost protection also.

5. And if you travel the whole length of the Roman world, you will find this everywhere the case. Even in our second capital[7] some temples still exist, robbed of all honor, admittedly, but though they be but few out of very many, still they have not vanished from it completely. And it was with these gods to aid them that the Romans used to march against the foe, engage them in battle, conquer them and, as conquerors, grant the vanquished a condition of life better than that which they had before their defeat, removing their fears and allowing them a share in their own civic life.

8. You, then, have neither ordered the closure of temples nor banned entrance to them. From the temples and altars you have banished neither fire nor incense nor the offerings of other perfumes. But this black-robed tribe,[8] who eat more than elephants and, by the quantities of drink they consume, weary those that accompany their drinking with the singing of hymns, who hide these excesses under an artificially contrived pallor—these people, Sire, while the law yet remains in force, hasten to attack the temples with sticks and stones and bars

7. Constantinople.
8. Libanius identifies Christian monks by their dark robes. His characterization of monks as gluttons, drunkards, and hypocrites is, no doubt, a rhetorical strategy of derision and slander.

of iron, and in some cases, disdaining these, with hands and feet. Then utter desolation follows, with the stripping of roofs, the demolition of walls, the tearing down of statues, and the overthrow of altars, and the priests must either keep quiet or die. After demolishing one, they scurry to another, and to a third, and trophy is piled on trophy, in contravention of the law.

9. Such outrages occur even in the cities, but they are most common in the countryside. Many are the foes who perpetrate the separate attacks, but after their countless crimes this scattered rabble congregates and calls for a tally of their activities, and they are in disgrace unless they have committed the foulest outrage. So they sweep across the countryside like rivers in spate, and by ravaging the temples, they ravage the estates, for wherever they tear out a temple from an estate, that estate is blinded and lies murdered. Temples, Sire, are the soul of the countryside: they mark the beginning of its settlement, and have been passed down through many generations to the men of today.

10. In them the farming communities rest their hopes for husbands, wives, children, for their oxen and the soil they sow and plant. An estate that has suffered so has lost the inspiration of the peasantry together with their hopes, for they believe that their labour will be in vain once they are robbed of the gods who direct their labours to their due end. And if the land no longer enjoys the same care, neither can the yield match what it was before, and, if this be the case, the peasant is the poorer, and the revenue jeopardized, for whatever a man's willingness, surely his inability frustrates him.

11. So the outrages committed by these hooligans[9] against the

estates bear upon vital matters of state. They claim to be attacking the temples, but these attacks are a source of income, for, though some assail the shrines, others plunder the wretched peasantry of what they have, both the produce stored from the land and their stock; and the invaders depart with the loot from the places they have stormed. Others are not satisfied with this, but they appropriate the land too, claiming that what belongs to this or that body is temple property, and many a man has been robbed of his family acres on this false title. Others, again, claim to worship their god with fasting, and yet grow fat on the misfortunes of other folk. And if the victims of this looting come to the "pastor" in town—for that is the title they give to a fellow who is not all that he should be—if they come and tearfully recount their wrongs, this pastor commends the looters and sends the victims packing with the assurance that they are lucky to have got off so lightly.

12. Yet, Sire, these victims are your subjects too, and as workers are more useful than idlers, so are they more useful than their oppressors. These are as the bees, those the drones. And if they hear that an estate has something worth looting, it is straightaway involved in sacrifices and is committing all manner of crimes: an armed visitation is called for, and up come the justices, which is the term they use to describe these—for want of a better word—footpads, for footpads at least try not to be found out and they deny their misdeeds. Call one of them a footpad and you insult him. But this crew flaunt their excesses, boast of them, advertise them to those who are unaware of them, and claim that they should be rewarded.

9. Namely, the monks.

13. But it is nothing else than war in peacetime waged against the peasantry. Ill-usage at the hands of their fellows is no alleviation for their misfortunes, except for the fact that it is even worse that those allies they might normally have had in times of trouble are responsible for their experiencing the above-mentioned outrages in time of peace.

15. The assertion is, of course, that they were punishing those who offer sacrifice and so contravene the law that bans it. This assertion, Sire, is always a lie. None of these ignorant rustics is so impudent as to claim to be above the law, and when I say the law, I mean its formulator. Do you really believe that those who cringe even at the tax-collector's uniform would despise the emperor's majesty? Yet this was the argument so often put to Flavianus, but it was never proved—nor is it now.

16. Now look! I challenge the guardians of this law. Who has seen anyone out of all the persons you have dispossessed who has sacrificed on the altars in the manner forbidden by the law, whether you be young or old, man or woman, a fellow villager who disagrees with sacrifices to the gods, or any native of the neighbourhood? Spite and envy could provide reason enough for neighbours to start proceedings against them, but for all that neither from them nor from anywhere else has anyone come forward, nor will he, if he has any qualms about perjury—not to mention the flogging for it. So what basis is there for the charge, save the mere assertion that they have performed an illegal sacrifice? But this will not do for the emperor.

17. "They did not sacrifice, then?" will be the comment. Of course they did, but for a banquet, a dinner, a feast, and the oxen were slaughtered elsewhere: no altar received the blood

offering, no single part of the victim was burned, no offering of meal began the ceremony, nor did libations follow it. If people assemble in some beautiful spot, slaughter a calf or a sheep, or both, and boil or roast it, and then lie down on the ground and eat it, I do not see that they have broken the laws at all.

18. You, Sire, have put no legal ban on these acts. By banning the performance of one specific action you automatically permit everything else. So even if they were in the habit of drinking together amid the scent of every kind of incense, they broke no law, nor yet if in their toasts they sang hymns and invoked the gods, unless indeed you intend to use a man's private life as grounds for accusation.

19. It used to be the custom for country folk to assemble in large numbers at the homes of the village notables at holiday time, to make a sacrifice and then hold a feast. This they did while ever it was permitted to do so, and thereafter all the rest, with the exception of sacrifice, remained permissible. So, summoned on the usual day, they dutifully honored it and the shrine in a manner that involved no risk. That they also thought fit to offer sacrifice no single person has ever said or heard, alleged convincingly or believed.

20. But it is not their way, they will say, to hand a man over to execution, even though he be guilty of the most heinous crime. I forebear to mention the numbers they have murdered in their riotings in utter disregard of the name they share, in case such incidents be described as due to over-hasty action: but your expulsion of people who by their personal care provided relief for poverty among old men and women and fatherless children, the majority of them suffering from severe physical handicaps—is not this murder? Isn't it execution? Isn't this

sentencing them to death, and to a death worse than ever, by starvation? For when their means of support have gone, this surely is the fate in store for them. Then in massacring their protectors, you have been massacring these innocents; but you wouldn't dream of doing so if they had broken the law! This bypassing of the courts of law is proof that their victims did not offer sacrifice. This killing without trial is a confession that there are no good grounds to try them.

21. And if they prate to me of the teachings of the scriptures that they profess to obey, I will counter them with the despicable acts they have committed. If this were not so, they would not be living on the fat of the land. As it is, we know how they spend their days—and their nights. How improbable it is for those who have no qualms about that to be so punctilious about this! In estate after estate, shrine after shrine has been wiped out by their insolence, violence, greed, and deliberate lack of self-control.

27. If such conversion could be effected simply by the destruction of temples, they would have been destroyed long ago by your decree, for you would long since have been glad to see this conversion. But you knew that you could not, and so you never laid a finger on these shrines. These people, even if they looked forward to some such result, ought to have advanced towards it in step with you and should have let the emperor share in their ambition. It would have been better, surely, to succeed in their objective by staying on the right side of the law rather than by abusing it.

28. And if they tell you that some other people have been converted by such measures and now share their religious beliefs, do not overlook the fact that they speak of conversions

apparent, not real. Their converts have not really been changed—they only say they have. This does not mean that they have exchanged one faith for another—only that this crew have been bamboozled. They go to their ceremonies, join their crowds, go everywhere where these do, but when they adopt an attitude of prayer, they either invoke no god at all or else they invoke the gods. It is no proper invocation from such a place, but it is an invocation for all that. In plays, the actor who takes the part of a tyrant is not a tyrant, but just the same as he was before putting on the mask: so here, everyone keeps himself unchanged, but he lets them think he has been changed.

29. Now what advantage have they won when adherence to their doctrine is a matter of words and the reality is absent? Persuasion is required in such matters, not constraint. If persuasion fails and constraint is employed, nothing has been accomplished, though you think it has. It is said that in their very own rules it does not appear but that persuasion meets with approval and compulsion is deplored. Then why these frantic attacks on the temples, if you cannot persuade and must needs resort to force? In this way you would obviously be breaking your own rules.

33. And the most crucial point of all—those who appear to have been our chief opponents in this particular have honored the gods even against their will. And who might these be? Why, those who have not dared rob Rome of its sacrifices. Yet, if all this business of sacrifice is nonsense, then why has not the nonsense been stopped? If it is harmful, then isn't this all the more reason? But if the stability of empire depends on the sacrifices performed there, we must consider that sacrifice is

everywhere to our advantage; the gods in Rome grant greater blessings, and those in the countryside and the other cities lesser ones; but any sensible man would welcome even such as these.

43. Temples, like other things, are imperial property. Look! when anyone causes what is his own to founder, is he behaving properly? Any man who hurls his purse into the sea is out of his mind: if the pilot cuts the cable on which the safety of his ship depends, or bids the sailor jettison his oar, he would be thought a lunatic. If a magistrate diminishes a city by however little, is he its great benefactor? What need to destroy what can be applied to another use? It is surely disgraceful for an army to wage war upon stones of its own, and for the general in charge to direct it against towering structures, erected long ago with great zeal, whose completion was the occasion for a festival for monarchs of yester-year.

49. And if we approach them and ask them to explain what they are up to, they disclaim any responsibility: their reply is that they have done as the emperor decreed and that he is the one to provide an explanation, and so on. But they should provide it, they who can never justify their behavior. Indeed, what justification could there be for such misdeeds? In public they disclaim such responsibility, but in private conclave with you they claim that none of their other actions has served your house so well. May the powers that have placed your person in authority over land and sea deliver your house from such service! You could receive no greater gift from them, for these self-styled friends and protectors, by their hurtful counsel and by employing your confidence to occasion hurt, have had no difficulty in harming you.

50. But I will cross-examine them, to demonstrate their guilt from the account I have just given. "Tell me: What is your reason for demolishing this great temple? That it was the emperor's decree? All right! Then those who destroyed it did nothing criminal because they did as the emperor decreed. So if anyone has done what the emperor has not decreed, he is a criminal, then? Well, you fall precisely into this category, for you have no such excuse to offer for your actions.

51. "And tell me! Why is the temple of Fortune here still intact, and that of Zeus, Athena and Dionysus? Because you wanted them to remain so? No, but because no one has given you the authority to move against them. But have you received any authority against those that you have destroyed? No! Then why should you not be punished? How can you describe your action as the imposition of a punishment when the victims in no single particular have done anything that could be described as a crime?"

52. You could have issued an edict, Sire: "Let none of my subjects revere or honor the gods, or invoke them for any blessing either for himself or for his children, save in silence and in secret. Let everyone worship the one that I adore,[10] go share in His rites, pray as He did, and bow his head under the hand of the Director of the people. And any who disobeys must die."

53. It would have been easy for for you to promulgate such an edict, yet you have refused to do so, nor have you imposed this yoke upon the conscience of men. You regard your religion as better than the other, but that is no act of impiety nor yet

10. That is to say, Christ.

just cause for punishment either. Nor have you excluded its adherents from advancement, but you have given them office and made them your companions at table, and often too, you have drunk their health, and even now, in addition to other individuals, you have linked them to yourself, in the belief that it is to the benefit of the crown, a man who takes his oath by the gods in the presence of others and yourself. Nor do you take it amiss and conceive such oaths to be an offense against yourself, nor do you regard one who places his higher hopes in the gods as being necessarily evil.

54. You do not persecute us any more than he who harried the Persians by force of arms and persecuted those of his subjects whose religious beliefs differed from his own.[11] Then why do these people persecute us? By what right do they launch their attacks? How is it that they extend their furious grasp to the estates of others, and wreak destruction, or pillage and loot, and add insult to injury by boasting of their exploits?

55. If, Sire, you commend and command such actions, we will put up with them, not without sorrow, but we will demonstrate that we have been schooled to obedience. But if these people without your permission proceed to attack anything that has escaped them or has been hastily restored, you may be sure that the landowners will defend both themselves and the law.

XI. Ambrose's and Symmachus's Petitions to the Emperor Valentinian Concerning the Altar of Victory (c. 389 CE)

Libanius, while arguing for protection for the temples in his surroundings, had believed the temples and altars in Rome to be secure. That was, however, only qualifiedly the case, as the removal of

11. Libanius here makes reference to Julian, the last non-Christian emperor.

the altar of the goddess Victory from the steps of the Roman Senate building under the Emperor Gratian (375–383 CE) shows. Symmachus, a Roman senator and prefect of the city of Rome, had appealed to Gratian on several occasions to restore the altar, albeit without success, and now renewed his petition to the Emperor Valentinian. His request and Ambrose's reply reveal the different ways in which Christians and pagans framed their arguments for religious dominance and toleration, and the ongoing debate over the Christianization of the Empire.

Symmachus, *Relatio* III

Submission of Symmachus, Prefect of Rome.

1. As soon as the most noble senate, ever your loyal subject, noted that crimes were being subjected to laws, and observed that pious princes were cleansing the notoriety of recent times, it was moved by inspiration of this happy age to belch out a long-suppressed grief, and it has instructed me as envoy to convey its grievances for a second time, after an audience with the late emperor had been refused me by disreputable men, precisely because otherwise justice would not have failed me, my lords and emperors Valentinian, Theodosius and Arcadius, glorious, victorious, and triumphant, ever Augusti.

2. I am therefore performing a twofold duty: as your prefect I am attending to public business, and as envoy I am delivering the instructions given me by my fellow citizens. There is no conflict of interests here. For men have now ceased to think that they can prevail through the support of men at court if their views are unrepresentative. To be loved, to be courted, to be treated with affection, now counts for more with the imperial power. Who could bear it if private quarrels were

found to have harmed the public good? The senate rightly attacks those who have given their own power precedence over the reputation of the prince. It is our work to keep watch on behalf of Your Clemency. If we defend the customs of our ancestors, the laws and destiny of our country, what stands to gain more than the glory of the present age, glory which will be all the greater when you realize that you have no license to do anything that is contrary to the custom of our forbears?

3. So that is why we ask you to give us back that status of religion, which has been of benefit to our commonwealth for so long. At any rate let us "count the emperors,"[12] emperors who belong to either school, to either persuasion.[13] The earlier rulers practiced the rites of our fathers; the more recent did not abolish them. If the piety of the old does not provide a precedent, let the policy of turning a blind eye of the more recent ones do so. Who is on such good terms with the barbarians as not to need the Altar of Victory? We are apprehensive about the future, and therefore avoid omens of that kind. If the honor has been denied to the divinity, let it at least once more be paid to her name. For Your Eternity owes much to Victory, and will owe more still. Let those men shun this power, who have gained no benefits from her. But as for you, do not reject the patronage, which favors our triumphs. Everybody devoutly desires to possess this force. Nobody should deny that it is right to venerate a force which he admits to be exceedingly desirable.

4. But even supposing that it would have been wrong to refrain

12. Symmachus here refers to the call "Count the senators!" by which a senator who disagreed with a decision and did not believe it to have the support of a senate majority would call for a vote.

13. That is to say, Christianity or paganism.

from causing this bad omen, surely it was fitting at least not to lay hands on the decorations of the senate chamber. Permit us old men, I beg you, to transmit to our descendants what was passed on to us when we were boys. Love of tradition is a great thing. It was altogether right that that act of the deified [Emperor] Constantius did not remain in force for long. You should refrain from following any precedent which you know to have been soon abolished. We are concerned for the perpetuity of your reputation and name, to make sure that a future generation will find nothing to criticize.

5. Where are we to swear to observe your laws and decrees? What religious sanction will deter the dishonest mind from lying when giving evidence? All things are full of God, and nowhere are perjurers safe; but the mere presence of religion can be a very powerful deterrent to wrongdoing. That altar sustains the harmonious unity of all the senate. That altar strengthens the good faith of each individual, and nothing contributes more to the authority of our decisions than that the house reaches all decisions, as it were, under oath. So our deconsecrated chamber will lie wide open to perjury. Can it really be that my noble emperors, whose safety depends on a public oath of loyalty, will judge this state of affairs to be acceptable?

6. But the deified Constantius, it is argued, did the same. Then let us rather imitate other actions of that emperor. He would surely not have attempted anything of that kind, if somebody else had already made that mistake before him. For a mistake on the part of a predecessor is a lesson to the successor, and censure of past error leads to its being corrected. It was perfectly right for the ancestor of Your Clemency not to shrink

from giving offense in an unprecedented situation. Surely it is not proper for us to use the same excuse, if we imitate an act that we remember to have met with disapproval?

7. Let Your Eternity be reminded of other actions of the same emperor, which are more worthy of your imitation. He did not take away any of the privileges of the Vestal Virgins. He filled up the priestly colleges with men of noble birth. He did not deny their expenses to the rites of the Roman state, and following a joyful senate through all the streets of the eternal city, he gazed on the shrines with serene expression, read the names of the gods inscribed on their gables, inquired after the origins of the temples, expressed admiration of their founders, and while he himself followed different rites, he preserved these for the empire.

8. For everyone's customs, everyone's cults are his own. The divine mind assigned different cults to different cities to be their protectors. As souls are assigned to men at birth, so guardian spirits are allotted to peoples to rule their destinies. There is also the fact of utility, which more than anything else convinces men that gods exist. For since reason is totally in the dark, surely knowledge of the gods comes to us most directly through memory and records of past success. If long passage of time gives religious practices their authority, we must keep faith with so many centuries, and we must follow our parents as they prosperously followed theirs.

9. Let us now suppose that Rome herself is standing here in your presence, and is addressing you with these words: "Best of emperors, fathers of your country, have respect for my years, which pious observance of our rites has given me. Allow me to live by the ancestral ceremonies, for I do not repent of them.

Let me live by my own custom; I am, after all, freeborn. This worship subjected the world to my laws. These sacrifices drove Hannibal from my walls and the Senones from the Capitol. Was I then only preserved for this, that I should be scolded as a very old woman?

10. "I needs will see what kind of innovation it is that they think must be introduced; but to make old age to change its ways is both too late, and humiliating." Is that why we now ask for peace for the gods of our fathers, our native gods? It is reasonable to think that whatever is worshipped by each of us is ultimately the same. We look at the same stars. We share the sky. The same universe surrounds us. What does it matter with what philosophy each individual seeks for the truth? It is not possible to reach so great a secret by a single route. But that is a topic for leisured academic discussion. It is prayers that we are offering you now, not debating points.

11. What profit did your sacred treasury derive from withdrawing the privileges of the Vestal Virgins? Are the most generous of emperors withdrawing what even the most niggardly have granted? Honor is the only thing they gain as a result of those privileges, which are, as it were, their wages for chastity: that they have immunity from public duties is considered the badge of honor of their priesthood, just as their headbands are an ornament of their heads. They ask for only the bare title of the privilege, since they are protected from actual expenditure because of their poverty. So the people who deprive them of material possessions actually contribute rather more to their reputation. For virginity dedicated to the public good grows in merit when it is without reward.

12. The integrity of your treasury should have nothing to do

with income of this kind. The exchequer of good emperors ought not to be filled at the expense of priests, but with plunder from enemies. Can any amount of profit compensate for the odium? Yet avarice is not in accord with your character. This fact makes those who are deprived of their ancient subsidies even more unhappy. For under emperors who keep their hands from other people's property, who fight against their own greed, an exaction which is not motivated by the covetousness of the exactor has no other purpose than to damage the victim.

13. In addition the exchequer retains lands left to the Virgins and ministers of religion in accordance with the wishes of the dying.[14] I beg you, who are the priests of justice, that the right to succeed to private legacies be restored to the cults of your city. Let men dictate their wills free from worry, and let them know that under emperors who are not rapacious, what they have written will stand. Allow the human race to enjoy that happiness, and let it bring joy to you also. The precedent of this case is beginning to worry the dying. Shall it be said that Roman law does not apply to Roman religious institutions? What should one call the seizure of properties which no law, no crisis has made forfeit?

14. Freedmen receive legacies. Appropriate benefits under the terms of a will are not denied to slaves. Only Virgins of noble birth, and the ministers of the sacred rites linked to our destiny, are excluded from properties that are theirs by the rights of inheritance. What is the advantage of dedicating one's virginity to the public safety, and of giving to the eternity of the empire the support of heavenly protection, of conciliating

14. Some Romans had historically left testamentary bequests to the Vestals.

friendly powers to watch over your armies and your eagles, of undertaking effective vows for the benefit of all, yet not to share with all the protection of law? And so even the condition of a slave, bound to the service of men, is preferable. We are damaging the state, which never benefits from ingratitude.

15. Let no one imagine that I am defending the cause of religion alone. From evil deeds of this kind have sprung all disasters of the Roman race. The law of our parents honored the Vestal Virgins and the ministers of the gods with a modest living and deserved privileges. This endowment remained unaltered until the time of the corrupt moneychangers who diverted the allowances owed to holy chastity to pay the wages of the lowly dock-workers. This action was followed by a general famine, and a scanty harvest disappointed the expectations of all.

16. This is not the fault of the soil. We do not blame the scorching south wind. Rust did not injure the crops, nor did weeds kill the corn. The year's produce was dried up by sacrilege. It was inevitable that what was being denied to religious obligations would be lost to all. If there is any parallel to this calamity, by any means let us attribute even this great famine to annual variation; but the cause that produced crop failure as extensive as this must be very grave indeed. Bushes in the forest are keeping people alive, and the country folk in their need have once again resorted to the trees of Dodona.[15]

17. Did the provinces ever suffer anything of this kind while public emolument was feeding the ministers of religion? When were oaks shaken for human consumption, when were the roots of plants torn up, when did it happen that mutually

15. That is to say, to living on acorns. Dodona was the location of a famous oak tree.

dependent regions were unable to make up each other's shortage through borrowed fertility, as long as sacred virgins shared the free corn supply of the Roman people? The public provision for the priests promoted the fertility of the soil: it was an aid to productivity rather than a hand-out. Can there be any doubt that a gift has always provided plenty for all, when it [i.e., its withholding] is punished by shortage for all?

18. Someone will say that a public subsidy has been denied merely to the expenses of a foreign religion. May good emperors never take the view that what has in the past been assigned to particular individuals out of public funds remains at the disposal of the exchequer. For as the commonwealth is made up of individuals, so what is paid out by it again becomes the property of individuals. Your rule governs everything, but you safeguard for each his own, and with you justice prevails over license. At least consult your own generous feelings whether what you have transferred to others is still to be considered public property. Resources once and for all donated to honor our city cease to belong to those who have donated them, and what at the outset was a free gift becomes by time and usage an entitlement.

19. If anybody insists that, unless you take on yourself the odium of those who are now withdrawing the donation, you are conniving with those who originally made it, he is trying to intimidate your mind with a fear that is groundless. May the mysterious guardians of all the sects be gracious to Your Clemency, and especially they who in the past helped your ancestors. May they defend you! May they be worshipped by us! We plead for the return of that establishment of religion which preserved the empire for the deified father of Your

Highness, which furnished an emperor enjoying good fortune and legitimate heirs.

20. From his citadel in the sky, the senior deified looks down on the tears of the priests, and thinks that he personally is being criticized by the abolition of a practice which he had gladly preserved. Do a favor also to your deified brother, and by correcting a policy that was not his own, hide an act which, unknown to him, had offended the senate. For it is agreed that the embassy was denied access precisely so that he should not hear the judgement of the council of state. You will therefore be furthering the reputation of earlier times, if you do not hesitate to abolish an act that needs to be shown not to have been that of an emperor.

Ambrose, Ep. 72 (17)

Bishop Ambrose, to the most blessed *princeps* and most Christian emperor Valentinian.

1. As all people that are under the dominion of Rome serve you, emperors and princes of this world, so you yourselves serve almighty God and the holy faith. There is no way that salvation can be assured other than that everyone truly worships the true God, that is, the God of the Christians, by whom all things are governed. For he alone is the true God, who is to be worshipped from the depths of our minds; "for the gods of the peoples are demons,"[16] the Scriptures say.

2. Now everyone is in the service of this true God, and he who undertakes to worship God with his innermost spirit offers him neither duplicity nor prevarication, but zeal and devotion to

16. Ps. 96:5.

the faith. And if he does not go as far as that, he at least ought not to display any sympathy with worship of idols and the rites of impious ceremonies. For nobody deceives God to whom all secrets, even of the heart, are crystal clear.

3. And so, seeing that you, most Christian Emperor, are duty bound to display your faith to the true God, along with enthusiasm for that faith, care and dedication, I am surprised that some people have conceived the hope that you are duty bound to order the restoration of altars to pagan deities, as well as to provide money for the expenses of impious sacrifices. For if you give funds that have already for a long time been claimed by the *fiscus* or the *arca*,[17] it will not be thought that you are only restoring to them what was theirs, but rather that you are bestowing what is your own.

4. And the people who are now complaining of their expenses are the same men who never spared our blood, who demolished the very walls of our churches from the foundations. The same people who, by a law of Julian, not long ago denied our spokesmen the right of speaking and teaching, which is common to all,[18] now also ask you for privileges, for privileges moreover which have frequently been used to entrap Christians. For their scheme was to ensnare large numbers of people by means of these privileges, exploiting the carelessness of some and the anxiety of others to avoid disagreeable public duties. And because not all men prove strong, a substantial number lapsed, even under Christian emperors.

17. The precise reference is unclear, but Ambrose here seems to refer to two Roman treasuries.
18. Ambrose here refers to Emperor Julian's attempt to deny Christians access to higher education.

5. Even if these privileges had not been withdrawn already, I would show you that they ought to be abolished at your command. But seeing that they have been curtailed or forbidden over almost the whole world by several previous emperors, and that at Rome Gratian of august memory, the brother of Your Clemency, withdrew them for the sake of the true faith, publishing rescripts to repeal them, do not, I beg you, tear down what has been decided in accordance with our faith; do not annul your brother's orders. If he has made any ruling in any secular matters, nobody thinks that these may be disregarded, so is an order involving religion now to be trodden underfoot?

6. Let no one creep up on your youthful age. If it is a pagan [as in this case] who makes these demands, he should not bind your mind with the fetters of his superstition, but that enthusiasm of his should teach and admonish you with what enthusiasm you ought to show zeal for the true faith, seeing that he defends something totally devoid of truth with such passion. I too urge that deference be shown to the merits of famous men, but one thing is certain: God must be preferred to all men.

7. When there is to be a discussion of a military matter we should seek the opinion of a man experienced in battles. We should accept his advice. When the issue concerns religion, think about God. No man is slighted when almighty God is preferred to him. That man has his opinion. You do not force a man to worship against his will what he refuses to worship. So you yourself, Emperor, must be allowed the same freedom! And everyone must bear it with patience, if he cannot extort from the emperor something that he would greatly resent if

the emperor wanted to extort it from himself. The attitude of a turncoat is as a rule disliked even by pagans. Everybody ought to be free to defend the sincere conviction of his mind, and to hold on to it.

8. But if any calling themselves Christians think that you ought to decree anything of that kind, do not let their meaningless words win over your mind, or their hollow claims deceive you. Whoever speaks in favor of this, as does he who decrees it, is in effect offering a pagan sacrifice. Even so, a sacrifice by one individual is preferable to the falling away of all. For in this case the whole Christian senate is at risk.

9. If today, which God forbid, some pagan emperor were to set up an altar to idols, and to compel Christians to assemble to be present when men are offering sacrifice, so that ash from the altar, cinders from the sacrilege, smoke from the pyre would fill the breath and mouths of the faithful; and if in that chamber he [the emperor] were to make a proposal on which they were compelled to vote under oath at the altar of the idol (for as they explain, it was precisely for this purpose that an altar was placed in the *curia*, so that, influenced—as they think—by its oath, each session of the senate would deliberate honestly for the common good, even though the senate is now filled with a majority of Christians), under these circumstances a Christian, obliged to take part in a session of the senate, would consider that he was being persecuted; and this situation does sometimes happen, for they are compelled to attend, even by threat of sanctions. So while you are emperor, will Christians actually be forced to swear at the altar? What is the meaning of swearing an oath, if not to acknowledge the divine power of him whom you invoke as guarantor of your

truthfulness? While you are emperor, does somebody actually ask and demand that you order the setting up of an altar, and the granting of money for impious sacrifices?

10. But this cannot be decreed without sacrilege. I therefore ask you not to decree it, not to make such an order, not to put your name under any such decree. As a bishop of Christ, I appeal to your faith. All of us bishops would have joined me in the appeal, if the report which reached men's ears, that something of the kind had either been proposed in your consistory or petitioned by the senate, had not been so incredible and sudden. But let it not be said that this is a petition of the senate: a handful of pagans are exploiting the title they all share. For about two years ago, when they were trying to make the same petition, the holy Damasus, bishop of the Roman Church, chosen by the judgement of God, sent me a memorandum which the Christian senators—and they were innumerable—had given him, insisting that they had authorized nothing of that kind, that they did not agree with that kind of petition of the pagans, that they were not giving their consent; complaining both publicly and privately that they would not attend the senate, if any decree of that kind was issued. Is it then worthy of your times, which are Christian times, that the dignity of Christian senators should be slighted, so that pagan senators might have their profane purpose gratified? I passed on the memorandum to the brother of Your Clemency, on the basis of which it was certain that it was not the senate, as a whole, which had given instructions to the envoys in the matter of the cost of the rites of superstition.

11. But perhaps it will be said, "Why then were they [the Christian senators] not present in the senate when these

petitions were recently drawn up?" Surely the men who stayed away express their views clearly enough. Those who spoke before the emperor have spoken clearly enough. And do we wonder that they [the pagan senators] are depriving private individuals at Rome of the freedom to oppose them, seeing that they will not allow you to be free to refuse to command something of which you disapprove, and so to remain true to your own beliefs?

12. And thus, remembering the embassy that was recently entrusted to me, I once more appeal to your faith; I appeal to your feelings: do not decide that you must reply favorably to this kind of pagan petition, nor commit the sacrilege of attaching your signature to such a reply. At any rate refer the matter to the father of your Piety, the *princeps* Theodosius, whom you are accustomed to consult in all matters of greater importance. There is nothing of greater importance than religion, nothing more exalted than faith.

13. If this were a civil case, the right to reply would be reserved for the opposing party. This is a case of religion. As bishop I appeal to you: let me be given a copy of the communication that was submitted, so that I can make a fuller refutation, and subsequently let the father of Your Clemency, when consulted about the whole issue, deign to produce a reply. But it is certain that if the decision goes the other way, we the bishops will not be able to bear it with indifference, and pretend that nothing has happened. You will still be free to come to church, but when you get there you will find no bishop, or you will find one who will resist you.

14. What will you reply to a bishop who says to you, "The church does not want your gifts, because with your gifts you

have adorned temples of the pagans. The altar of Christ rejects your offerings with contempt, because you have built an altar for graven images. The voice, the hand and the signature are yours: the act is yours. The Lord Jesus refuses and rejects your allegiance, because you have given your allegiance to idols: for he says to you, 'You cannot serve two masters.'[19] Virgins consecrated to God lack your privileges, yet the Vestal Virgins claim them. Why do you look for priests of God when you have overruled them in favor of the profane petitions of pagans? We cannot enter into fellowship with pagan error."

15. What will you reply to these words? That you are a boy, and that you have lapsed? Every age is mature where Christ is concerned. Every age has the full experience of God. A childhood of faith is not recognized. Even young children have confessed Christ speaking fearlessly in the face of persecutors. What will you reply to your brother?[20] Surely he will say to you, "I did not think that I had been defeated, because I left you as emperor. I was not sorry to die, because I had you as my heir. I did not grieve at abandoning power, because I believed that my decrees, above all those related to the divine religion, would remain throughout all ages. These triumphal inscriptions of devoted virtue I had set up. This was the booty of a victory over the world, the plunder won from the devil, the spoils taken from the enemy of mankind, which I was offering up to commemorate a victory which is eternal. Of what more could my enemy have robbed me? You have abolished my decrees, which so far he who rebelled against me has not done. Now a more painful weapon is piercing my body, for it is my brother who is condemning my laws. Your act is endangering the

19. Matt. 6:24.
20. Emperor Gratian, who had removed the Altar of Victory from the Senate in the first place.

better part of me. My death was the death of my body; this is the death of the good I have done. It is only now that my empire is being annulled, and what is more painful, it is being annulled by your followers and annulled by mine, and precisely those acts are being annulled for which even my adversaries have praised me. If you have acquiesced willingly, you have condemned my faith; if you have yielded against your will, you have betrayed your own. And so to make things worse, my danger is added to yours."

16. Again, what will you reply to your father,[21] who will appeal to you with greater sorrow, saying, "You have completely misjudged me in thinking that I collaborated with the pagans. Nobody reported to me that there was an altar in that Roman senate house. I never believed that there could be such wickedness, that pagans should offer sacrifice in the council shared by Christians and pagans alike, that pagans should insult the Christians present, and that Christians should be compelled to be present at sacrifices against their will. Many and various crimes were committed while I was emperor. I punished all that were discovered. If at that time anybody avoided detection, does this give him the right to claim that I approved of something which nobody had reported to me? Your assessment of me is as wrong as it could be, if [you think] that pagan superstition and not my own faith preserved the empire for me."

17. And so, Emperor, realizing that by issuing such a decree you would be wronging first of all God, but also your father and your brother, take the action, I beg you, that you know will advance your salvation with God.

21. Emperor Valentinian I.

XII. Ambrose's Engagement with Emperors Constantius II and Theodosius

Ambrose, Ep. 76 (20)

Ambrose's Ep. 76 is an account, directed to his elder sister Marcellina, a consecrated virgin, of the so-called Basilica Controversy. Milan, Ambrose's city, in the 380s was also the domicile of the court of child-Emperor Constantius II and his mother, Justina. The latter were Christians, albeit of a variety that rejected the Nicene creed and its declaration of consubstantiality of Christ and the Father, ascribing rather a superior divinity to the Father. In the weeks leading up to Easter, the court sought to requisition one of the city's basilicas for its use as well as the use of other non-Nicene Christians. Ambrose refused and, along with his congregation, sought to occupy the city's churches, even in the face of military threat.

Ambrose to his sister Marcellina.

1. Since in almost all your letters you enquire anxiously about the state of the church, listen to what is going on. The day after I received your letter in front of and under the present cathedral, in which you revealed that your dreams were disturbing you, a mass of grave anxieties was set in motion. The demand now was not just for the Portiana, that is a church outside the walls, but for the New Basilica, one which is within the walls, and larger.

2. The first thing was that some men of [illustrious rank], counts of the imperial consistory, met me with the demand that I should both surrender the basilica, and see to it that the people did not cause any disturbance. I replied, correctly, that a temple belonging to God cannot be handed over by a bishop.

3. The following day there was an acclamation of support in the church. No less a man than the praetorian prefect arrived there. He started to urge us to withdraw at least from the Portian Basilica. The people protested. We parted, with the prefect saying that he would report to the emperor.

4. On the following day, which happened to be a Sunday, after the lessons and the sermon, when I had sent away the catechumens, I was teaching the Creed to a number of candidates for baptism in the basilica of the baptistery.[22] There I received the report that as soon as it became known that they had sent palace officials to the Basilica Portiana, and that they were putting up imperial hangings, a section of the people began to flock there. I stuck to my duty, however, and began to celebrate mass.

5. While I was making the offering, I learned that the people had made a prisoner of some man called Castulus, whom the Arians[23] call a priest. They happened to have come across him in the street on their way. Right in the middle of the offertory I started to weep bitter tears, and to beg God to come to our aid, and prevent anyone's blood being shed in an ecclesiastical dispute, or at least that it was my blood which would be shed, not only for the salvation of the people, but also on behalf of the Arians themselves. In short: I sent priests and deacons, and had the fellow snatched out of harm's way.

6. Thereupon very severe penalties were decreed, in the first

22. Familiarity with the Nicene creed as the major confession would have been an essential step toward baptism.
23. Subordinationist Christians who did not affirm the Nicene formula and the consubstantiality of Father and Son in the Trinity. Historically, if somewhat slanderously, they were frequently identified with Arius, a presbyter from Alexandria, whose conflict with the local bishop in the early decades of the fourth century touched off the debate over the shared essence and divinity of Christ and the Father.

place against the whole corporation of traders. And so during the holy days of the last week of Lent, a time when by custom debtors are freed from their shackles, there was a loud rattle of chains, chains being hung around the necks of people who had done nothing. Two hundred pounds by weight of gold was demanded, the entire sum to be paid within three days. Their response was that they would give as much again, or double if that were demanded, provided only they were allowed to keep their faith. The prisons were full of traders.

7. All the members of the Palatine departments, that is, the *memoriales*, the *agentes in rebus*, the subordinate officials of various counts, were under orders to abstain from appearing in public, on the ostensible grounds of being kept from involvement in a seditious assembly. The notables were threatened with many and grave consequences unless they surrendered the basilica. Persecution was raging, and it seemed that if they got the gate opened, they would break into every kind of atrocity.

8. I myself was being pressed by the counts and tribunes to agree to an immediate handover of the basilica. They said that the emperor was exercising his legal rights, since all things were subject to his authority. I replied that if he was after what belongs to me, that is, my land, my money, any right, no matter what, that was mine, I would not resist—even though everything of mine really belongs to the poor. But the things that are God's, I insisted, were not subject to the power of the emperor. "If my family property is what is wanted, come and take it; if my person, I will offer it. Do you want to drag me off to prison? Or to execution? I am ready. I will not surround myself with a defensive wall of my people, nor will I cling to

the altar, begging for my life: much more gladly, in defending the altar, I will become a sacrifice."

9. Yes, I was terrified when I learned that military men had been sent to seize the basilica of the church, for I feared that their appropriation of the basilica would be accompanied by carnage, which would result in the ruin of the city as a whole. I kept praying that I might not survive the cremation of so great a city, perhaps of all Italy. I shrank from the odium of being the cause of bloodshed. I offered my own throat. Some tribunes of the Goths were standing close by. I assailed them saying: "Was it for this that the Roman Empire admitted you, that you should offer yourselves as agents for the promotion of civil strife? To where will you emigrate if this region is destroyed?"

10. I was called upon to pacify the people. I replied that it was in my power not to rouse them, but to pacify them lay with God. After all, if the emperor really believed that I was the instigator, he ought to have me punished straight away, or to have me transported to whatever desolate part of the world he pleased. On my saying this, they departed. I spent the whole day in the Old Basilica. From there I took myself home, to rest, so that if anybody wished to deport me he would find me ready.

11. The next morning before dawn, just as I had set foot outside my doorstep, the basilica was occupied by the troops that had surrounded it. The word was that the military enjoined on the emperor that if he wished to come out [to attend church], he would have the opportunity. They themselves, however, would attend him only if they saw that he was associating with the

Catholics;[24] otherwise they would go over to the crowd called by Ambrose.

12. Not one of the Arians was brave enough to come out, since there were none of the citizens there, a few from the imperial household, and a number of Goths. At one time wagons were homes to these people, so now their wagon is the church. Wherever that woman makes her way she drags with her a swarm of followers.

13. I could tell from the groans of the people that the church was surrounded. But during the reading of the lesson word was brought to me that the Basilica Nova too was filling up with our people; the crowd seemed bigger than when they had not been under duress; a shout had gone up for a Reader. To be brief: the very soldiers who appeared to have taken possession of the basilica, learning that I had given instruction that they were to be kept from joining the congregation in the Eucharist, started to come here to our service. At the sight of them there was panic among the women; one of them rushed forward. The soldiers themselves, however, were declaring that they had come to prayer, not to battle. The people raised a cheer. They kept demanding—with such restraint, with such steadfastness, with such loyalty—that we should march to that other basilica. In that basilica too, it was said, the people were demanding my presence.

14. Then I began the following sermon: "My children, you have heard the Book of Job being read, which is regularly read at this service on this day. The devil himself was well aware from

24. That is to say, those who identified with the pro-Nicene faction, which laid claim to representing Christianity as it had been practiced and confessed everywhere, from the beginning of the Church.

experience that that book would be publicized in which the whole armory of his artifices is revealed and exposed. That is why he has bestirred himself against us all the more forcefully today. But thanks be to our God, who has made you so strong in faith and patience. I mounted the pulpit to marvel at Job, and found all of you Jobs to marvel over. Job lives again in everyone of you; out of each one of you the patience and virtue of that holy man shine brightly. For what could be said by Christians that is more apposite than what has been spoken today by the Holy Spirit through you: 'We are asking you to think again, Augustus; we are not being aggressive. We are not afraid, but we are asking you to think again.' This is what befits Christians, to strive for the serenity of peace, and not to allow steadfastness for the faith and for truth to be overcome by fear of death. For God is our patron, who will save those who hope in him.

15. "But let us come to the readings before us. You see license is given to the devil to test us, so that the virtuous may prove themselves.[25] The evil one envies good men making progress in virtue, and tests them out in all sorts of ways. He tested out the holy Job through his ancestral possessions, he tested him out through his sons, he tested him out through bodily pain.[26] A strong man is tested through his own physical suffering, a weaker man through another's. From me too he wanted to take away my riches which I possess in you, and he desired to squander that inheritance represented by your serenity. And you too, my good sons, he was eager to snatch from me, you for whom I daily renew the sacrifice. He was trying to entangle you in the fallout of the ruins of a public uprising. I have therefore

25. Job 1:12.
26. Job 2:7.

already experienced two kinds of trial. And perhaps because the Lord God knows me to be rather weak he has not yet given [the devil] power over my body. Even though I desire it, even though I offer myself, he perhaps still judges me unequal to that contest, and he exercises me with labors of a different kind. Nor did Job begin with that contest, but he finished with it.

16. "But Job was tested by bad news heaped on bad news; he was also tested by the woman who said, 'Speak some word against God and die.'[27] Do you observe how many trials are now suddenly launched against me? Goths, weapons, federate troops, the merchants fined, and the saints punished. Do you realize what is being ordered when the instruction is given, 'Surrender the basilica?' It is the equivalent of 'Speak some word against God and die'; and not just 'Speak against God' but 'Take action against God.' The instructions are 'surrender the altar of God.'

17. "So we are harassed by imperial edicts but we are fortified by words of the Bible, which enable us to give the reply: 'You have spoken like one of the foolish women.'[28] This testing is therefore no easy thing, for we know that trials and temptations issuing through women are particularly severe. After all Eve tripped up even Adam, and that is how he came to disobey the instructions of heaven. When Adam discovered his mistake, and his guilty conscience was accusing him, he longed to hide. But it was impossible for him to hide, and so God said to him, 'Adam, where are you?' which is the same as 'Where have you been? Where are you now? Where had I

27. Job 2:9.
28. Job 2:10.

placed you? Where have you strayed?' You know that you are naked, because you have lost the covering of the good faith. Those objects with which you are trying to cover yourself are leaves. Having rejected the fruit, you are anxious to hide under the leaves of the law. But you will be found out. For the sake of one woman you have chosen to abandon the Lord your God. That is why you now flee Him whom you previously sought to see. With one woman for company you have chosen to hide yourself away, and to abandon the mirror of the world, your dwelling in paradise, the grace of Christ.[29]

18. "Do I need to add that that Jezebel persecuted even Elijah most cruelly,[30] that Herodias had John the Baptist killed?[31] Particular women have been a trial for particular individuals. For myself, the trials are all the harder because my worth is so much less. My strength is weaker, my danger greater. One generation of women follows another. The objects of their hatred shift. Their intrigues change. Men in high positions are summoned to appear in court, and a charge of 'an insult to the emperor' is trumped up. What motive could there be for inflicting such a trial on a worm like me, unless it is not me but the church which they are persecuting?

19. "Finally, the order comes: 'Surrender the basilica!' I reply, 'Emperor, it is not lawful for me to surrender the basilica, nor is it right for you to receive it. No law entitles you to violate the house of a private individual; do you think that you may seize the house of God?' The argument put forward is that everything is permitted to the emperor, that the world is his. I

29. Ambrose here elaborates Job 3:8. The exposition of "evil women" throughout the Old Testament is designed to paint Empress Justina as similarly dangerous to the church.
30. 1 Kings 1.
31. Matthew 14.

reply, 'Do not make trouble for yourself, Emperor, by thinking that you have any sort of imperial right over things that are God's. Do not exalt yourself. If you wish to rule for any length of time, be subject to God. It is written: "What is God's to God, what is Caesar's to Caesar."[32] Palaces belong to the emperor, churches to the bishop. The jurisdiction entrusted to you is over public buildings, not over sacred ones.' The statement is repeated that the emperor had sent word: 'I too am entitled to have one basilica.' I reply, 'It is not lawful for you to have it. What business have you with an adulteress?' For she who is not married to Christ in lawful marriage is an adulteress."

20. While I was speaking about these events, it was brought to my attention that the imperial hangings had been folded away, and that the basilica had been filled with people, and that my presence was being demanded. Immediately I brought my sermon round to this. I said, "How lofty and profound are the prophecies of the Holy Spirit! You remember, brethren, the reading at Matins, which we then repeated with great sorrow of soul. It was: 'O God, the heathens have come into your inheritance.'[33] And heathens did indeed come, and very much worse than heathens: for it was Goths who came, and men of a variety of foreign tribes, and they came armed, and after placing a cordon around the basilica they occupied it.[34] At this we were grief-stricken, being unmindful of your profundity. But while our shortsightedness was contemplating one possibility, your grace was working towards another.

21. "The heathens did come, but in truth they have come into

32. Mark 12:17.
33. Ps. 79:1.
34. In Ambrose's era, much of the Roman army consisted of soldiers who had been recruited from the empire's northern neighbors, the Gothic tribes.

your inheritance, for the men who came as heathens have been made into Christians. The men who came to seize our inheritance have become the co-heirs of God. I have defenders, people whom I used to consider enemies; I possess allies, people whom I used to regard as opponents. The prophecy that David sang of the Lord Jesus has been fulfilled: 'His abode has been established in peace and he has broken the horns of the bows, the shield, sword and war.'[35] To whom do we owe this gift, to whom this achievement? To you, Lord Jesus! You saw armed men come to your temple, the people groaning in consequence. Over here are the people groaning, and gathering together in great numbers, so as not to give the impression that they were surrendering the basilica of God. Next there are soldiers commanded to use force. Death was before my eyes; but in order to stop mad fury being let loose between the two groups, you, Lord, thrust yourself between them, and you made the two parties one. You restrained the armed men, no doubt saying the words, '"What profit is there in my blood,"[36] if there is a rush to arms, if in my temple the trumpet of war is sounded?' All thanks therefore be to you, Christ! It was not a legate, nor an envoy, but you, Lord, who have saved your people. You have torn away my sackcloth and girded me with gladness."

22. I was saying these things, in surprise that the emperor's anger could be assuaged by the zeal of the soldiers, the protestations of the counts, and the entreaty of the people. At that point I received the news that a notary was on his way to convey the emperor's instructions. I withdrew a little; he divulged the instructions. "What were you thinking of,"

35. Ps. 76:3.
36. Ps. 30:9.

he said, "that you acted contrary to the emperor's wishes?" I replied, "I do not know what his wishes are, and I am not sure what rash act is claimed to have taken place." He said, "Why did you send priests to the basilica? If you are a usurper I want to know, so that I know what preparations to make against you." I replied, saying that I had done nothing to the disadvantage of the church. On hearing that the basilica had been occupied by soldiers, I had merely given vent to greater distress; and when many people were calling on me to go there, I had said, "Surrender the basilica I cannot, but participate in fighting I ought not." But after I had learned that the imperial hangings had been removed from the basilica, and when the people were demanding that I should go there, I sent some priests. I had refused to go myself, but said, "I trust in Christ, that the emperor himself will come over to our side."

23. [I continued to the notary,] "If that looks like the behavior of a usurper, I agree that I have arms—but only for the service of Christ. I have power—to make the emperor an offering of my body. Why would he have hesitated to strike, if he thought me a usurper? Under the old dispensation, monarchy was conferred by priests, and not usurped by force; and it is commonly said that emperors aspired to priesthood rather than priests to monarchy. Christ fled to avoid being made king. We have our personal 'usurper': weakness is the 'usurper' of the priest. 'When I become weak,' Paul said, 'then am I strong.'[37] But he against whom God has not raised up an adversary must take care not to conjure up a usurper against himself. Not even Maximus makes this claim that I am a usurper against Valentinian. In fact he complains that he was unable to invade Italy on account of the intervention of my

37. 2 Cor. 12:10.

embassy." I added that priests have never been usurpers, but they have often suffered from usurpers.

24. We spent the whole day in this sorrowful state. The imperial hangings were, however, torn by children at play. I was unable to return home, because the soldiers who were guarding the basilica were stationed all round it. Together with the brethren we recited psalms in the smaller basilica.

25. On the following day [Thursday, April 2], as is customary, the book of Jonah was read, and when it was finished I began the sermon with: "A book has been read, brethren, in which it is prophesied that sinners are returning to repentance." This was then interpreted to mean that we were to hope for the future in the present. I went on to say that this just man had been willing to incur (God's) displeasure rather than see, or even prophesy, the destruction of a city. And it was because that prophecy was so harsh that Jonah had been saddened even by the withering of a gourd. We also read that God asked the prophet, "Are you sad for a gourd?" Jonah had replied, "Sad." Then the Lord our God had said that if for him the withering of a gourd was sufficient grounds for grief, how much more ought he [God] to be concerned for the salvation of so large a people. And that is why he had cancelled the destruction he had prepared for all the city.

26. Soon after, the news came that the emperor had ordered the troops to withdraw from the basilica, and that the money which they had been fined was to be returned to the merchants. Imagine the happiness of all the assembly at this moment, the cheers of all the people, the thanksgiving! Now it was the day on which our Lord gave himself up for us, when we are released from penance in the church. Vying to bring the

news, soldiers rushing towards the altars made it known with kisses, the symbol of peace. Then I realized that God had indeed smitten the worm that came at dawn, so that the whole city might be saved.

27. This is what happened, and would that this were the end of the story: but that worse disturbances are on the way is implied by some very threatening words of the emperor. I am called a usurper and even worse than a usurper. For when the counts were beseeching the emperor to proceed to the church, and said that they were doing this at the request of the soldiers, he replied, "If Ambrose were to give you the order, you would hand me over to him in chains." Just imagine what we can expect after that pronouncement. The pronouncement horrified everybody, but some of his men are working him up.

28. Finally Calligonus too, the *praepositus sacri cubiculi*, with characteristic effrontery, dared to declare to me, "Do you treat Valentinian with contempt while I am above ground? I shall have your head!" I replied, "May God allow you to carry out what you are threatening. For I will suffer as befits a bishop; you will behave as befits a eunuch." I only pray that God may deflect these people away from the church, turn all their weapons on me, and quench their thirst with my blood.

Ambrose, Ep. 51 (*Epistula extra collectionem* 11)

Ep. 51, by contrast, depicts Ambrose's engagement with Emperor Theodosius. The latter had been a great friend and champion of Ambrose's. When Theodosius sought to receive the Eucharist at Milan, however, in the aftermath of a particularly violent strike against an uprising in another part of the Roman Empire, the bishop refused. This letter reflects Ambrose's demand for the emperor's public penance—a demand to which, other early Christian historians tell us, Theodosius in due course acceded.

Ambrose, bishop, to the most august Emperor Theodosius.

1. The memory of our long friendship is precious to me, and I recall with gratitude the benefits that your extreme benevolence has so frequently shown towards others because of my intercession on their behalf. Understand, then, that if I refused to meet you on your arrival, I who have always desired ardently to see you, it could not be because of some lack of thankfulness on my part. In as few words as possible, I intend to set before you the reasons for my actions.

2. I perceived that of all those in your court, I alone had been deprived of the natural right of hearing, with the added frustration of being deprived of my duty of speaking. It has often happened, in fact, that you have been disturbed because of the fact that certain decisions taken in your council have been made known to me. Thus, I have been deprived of a right common to all, and that in spite of the Lord's own words, "there is no secret so hidden that it will not be made known."[38] Therefore, out of respect for you, I have sought to obey your will. I decided that you would have no cause for displeasure on my account. I insisted that no imperial decrees be reported to me. In every situation where I am with others, I refuse to listen, lest those who seek a reputation for conniving be present. Or, I listen in such a way that, though my ears are open, my voice is held, so that I may not be able to repeat what I heard, lest harm be brought to those who might be suspected of indiscretion.

3. What can I do? Should I not hear? I cannot block my ears

38. Luke 8:17.

with the wax of ancient fables. Should I repeat what I have heard? I have to be on guard in my own speech, lest what I feared in your commands would be realized and some act of bloodshed would be committed. Should I then keep silence? But, then my conscience would be bound and I would be in the most wretched state of all, robbed of my voice. What would become of that text, "if a priest does not speak to one who has erred, that one will die in his sin. The priest will be liable to punishment since he did not admonish the errant one?"[39]

4. Listen to this, august Emperor. I cannot deny your zeal for the faith. I recognize that you fear God. But you have an impulsive nature which quickly becomes merciful, if anyone seeks to soothe you. If one should provoke you, you grow more vehement, with the result that you can scarcely control yourself. If no one is to calm you, then, at least, let no one excite you! I willingly entrust your temper to you. Control yourself and for the love of what is good and holy, conquer the impetuosity of your nature.

5. I prefer to make this recommendation to you, privately, rather than to provoke you in public by some chance deed of mine. So, I prefer to appear lacking in duty rather than in submission. I prefer that others should see in me less of the authority of the priesthood than that you should find me wanting in respect to you. I prefer these things so that, if your impetuosity be controlled, your ability to choose counsel would be firm. I plead illness as my excuse. It is severe, but will hardly be relieved except by lighter duties. Nevertheless, I would prefer to die than not await your arrival in two or three days.

39. Ezek. 3:18.

6. An event has occurred in the city of Thessaloniki which has had no equal in human history. I would not have been able to prevent that massacre, but in a thousand ways, I have previously tried to convince you of the atrocity of such a deed. You yourself, in revoking your order—too late—realized well its gravity. In no way could I water down the seriousness of such a crime. The news of the deed was first heard when the synod assembled for the arrival of the bishops of Gaul. There was not a single person unaffected. No one took it lightly. The fact that you were still in communion with Ambrose in no way absolved you from guilt. Public resentment is already aroused against the deed and would become more violent against me, if no one had said that it is absolutely necessary for you to be reconciled with our God.

7. Will you be ashamed, O Emperor, to act as did David, the prophet-king, ancestor of Christ's race according to the flesh? Nathan told him of a rich man with many flocks who took the one sheep of a poor man, in order to entertain a guest. Realizing that the story was directed at him, David cried out, "I have sinned against the Lord."[40] Therefore, do not become impatient if we say to you, "You have done what the prophet reproached David for doing." If you listen to me with a submissive heart, you will say, "I have sinned against the Lord." If you make your own these words of the royal prophet, "Come, let us adore the Lord and fall down before him; let us weep before the Lord who made us,"[41] then it will also be said to you, "The Lord remits your sin, because of your repentance, and you will not die."[42]

40. 2 Sam. 2:13.
41. Ps. 95:6.
42. 2 Sam. 12:13.

8. Again, after David had ordered his people to be counted, he had remorse of heart and said to the Lord, "I have sinned greatly in giving this command. Now, O Lord, remove the iniquity of your servant, because I have sinned grievously."[43] Again, the prophet Nathan was sent to him, offering him a choice of three penalties: three years of famine in the land, pursuit by his enemies for three months, or mortal pestilence throughout the land for three days. David answered, "These three things are equally difficult for me. Let me fall into the hand of the Lord, for his mercies are many. Let me not fall into the hands of men."[44] His fault consisted in wanting to know how many people belonged to him. He ought to have left that knowledge to the Lord alone.

9. When the plague struck the people on the very first day, at dinner time, David saw the angel striking the people down. He said, "I have sinned. I, the shepherd, have done wrong. What has this flock done? Rather, strike me and my father's house."[45] The Lord repented and ordered the angel to spare the people, but David was to offer sacrifice. At that time, sacrifices were offered for sins; now, the sacrifices are repentance and penance. Thus, David became acceptable to God because of his humility. It is not surprising that a man sins. What must be condemned is failure to recognize his sin and refusal to humble himself.

10. Holy Job, also a mighty man in this world, says, "I did not conceal my sin but have made it known before all the people."[46] Saul, the fierce king, was asked by Jonathan his son, "Do not sin

43. 2 Sam. 24:10.
44. 2 Sam. 24:14.
45. 2 Sam. 24:17.
46. Job 31:34 LXX.

against your servant David. Why do you sin against innocent blood by murdering David without reason?"[47] Although he was king, he would have sinned by killing the innocent. Even David, as king, when he heard that the innocent Abner had been slain by Joab, the commander of his army, said, "I and my kingdom are innocent now and forever of the blood of Abner, the son of Ner."[48] And he fasted, in grief.

11. If I write all this to you, it is not to humiliate you, but that the example of these kings might inspire you to remove this sin from your kingdom. You will do so only by humbling yourself before God. You are a man, subject to temptation. Conquer it! A sin cannot be removed except by tears and repentance. Neither angel nor archangel can atone for you. The Lord, who alone has the power to say, "I am with you,"[49] does not forgive us when we have sinned until we have done penance.

12. I come to urge, to plead, to exhort, to admonish you, to recall you to your duty. I suffer to see that you, who were an example of outstanding virtue, whose great clemency could scarcely bear the punishments of the guilty, do not grieve over the death of so many innocent people. You have known outstanding success in battle; you have been worthy of praise for other achievements. Still, your piety has always been the crown of all your works. The devil has envied this, your most prized possession. Conquer him, while you still have the means to do so. Do not add another sin to your present guilt by taking an attitude that has already harmed many.

13. As for myself, in all other matters I am a debtor to your

47. 1 Sam. 19:4-5.
48. 2 Sam. 3:28.
49. Matt. 28:20.

goodness. If I were haughty toward you, I would be ungrateful, for your goodness is greater than that of all other emperors and has been equalled only by one. I have no reason to be unrelenting toward you. But, I do have one fear. I would not dare to offer the sacrifice in your presence. If an act is not permissible when the blood of one person has been shed, can it be allowed when the blood of so great a number has been shed? No.

14. I am writing this with my own hand, so that you alone will read it. As truly as I desire that the Lord deliver me from all my tribulations, it is not by any man nor through a messenger from any man, but by a clear revelation that this prohibition has been imposed on me. I was deeply troubled the night that I was preparing to leave. It seemed to me that you came into the church, but I was forbidden to offer the sacrifice. I do not count other trials which I could have avoided in the past. I endured them, I think, for the love of you. May the Lord grant that this affair be settled peacefully! Our God warns us in many ways: by heavenly signs, by the precepts of prophets, even by the visions of sinners. He wills to make use of such things to make us understand that we should ask him to remove troubles from us, to give peace to rulers, to protect the faith and tranquillity of the church which has such need of emperors who are good and faithful Christians.

15. Surely, you wish to be approved by God. It is written, "There is a time for all things."[50] "It is time to act, O Lord."[51] "It is a time for mercy, O God."[52] You will make your offering when you have received authorization to do so, when your victim

50. Eccles. 3:1.
51. Ps. 119:126.
52. Ps. 69:13.

will be acceptable to God. Would I not be delighted to win the emperor's favor, by acting according to your will, if the case so allowed? A simple prayer is already a sacrifice. It brings pardon. The offering of the sacrifice would only offend God now. The first implies humility; the other contempt. God himself has indicated that he prefers obedience to his commandments more than sacrifices. He has proclaimed this; Moses announced it to his people; Paul preached it to all. You also, do what you know is most important at this time. "I prefer mercy and not sacrifice."[53] Are they who denounce their own sins not better Christians than they who seek to justify them? "He is just who begins his prayer as his own accuser."[54] The sinner who accuses himself is justified, but not he who glories in his sin.

16. Would to God, O Emperor, that I had trusted my own judgment more than your customary way of acting! I knew how quick you were to grant pardon, how quickly you revoked your orders. You had done it so often before! And, suddenly, the act was done and I was unable to prevent a deed which I was not able to foresee. Let us thank God who desires to chastise his servants lest they be lost. My task is that of the prophets; let yours be that of the saints.

17. Is not the father of Gratian dearer to me than my own eyes? The other sacred pledges of your devotion, your children, are also worthy of pardon. I refer to those whom I do not separate from you in my love. I love you, I cherish you, I embrace you with my prayers. If you trust me, do as I say. If not, forgive what I do. It is because God comes first in my life.

53. Matt. 9:13.
54. Prov. 18:17 LXX.

May you and your blessed children, in perfect happiness and prosperity, enjoy perpetual peace, O most august Emperor!

XIII. Augustine, *The City of God* (c. 410–425 CE)

Concerning the City of God, against the Pagans *is Augustine of Hippo's magnum opus, a work that took well over a decade to complete. Begun in the aftermath of the first sack of Rome by the Visigoths, Augustine here seeks to respond to anxieties among both Christians and their non-Christian neighbors that the city's invasion reflected divine punishment for abandoning the old Roman gods. In the first ten books, Augustine argues against such a presupposition: the pagan deities could not have protected the city and, as the second of five books seek to show, would not even do their adherents any good in the next life. In the second half of the work, parts of which are reproduced here, however, Augustine undertakes the remarkable task of renarrating human history through the lens of two cities or societies. One, the "city of God," has remained focused on God and journeys toward reunion with God in the heavenly Jerusalem; the other, the "earthly city," is focused only upon itself and its own pleasures. As such, it journeys toward its eternal destruction. Augustine traces the journeys of both cities from their antediluvian origins to their anticipated ends. The selections included here will give the reader a glimpse into the nature and interactions of these cities.*

Book 1. Preface: Augustine Outlines His Plan

In this work, my dearest son Marcellinus, I have taken up the task of defending the most glorious city of God, whether in the course of these present times when it is on pilgrimage among the ungodly, living by faith, or in the stability of its eternal home which it now awaits in patience, "until justice returns in judgment,"[55] but will finally attain, by virtue of its surpassing excellence, in ultimate victory and perfect peace. I have undertaken to defend it against those who prefer their own gods to its founder; and, in doing so, I will keep my promise and pay my debt to you. It is a massive work, and arduous, but "God is our helper."[56]

For I know very well what efforts are needed to persuade the proud how great the power of humility is. But by humility we reach a height—a height not grasped by human arrogance but granted by divine grace which transcends all these earthly pinnacles that totter with the shifts of time. For the king and founder of the city of which we are going to speak has made known, in the Scripture of his people, a provision of divine law which asserts "God resists the proud but gives grace to the humble."[57] This belongs to God alone, but the inflated spirit of human pride strives to claim it for itself and loves to have the same thing said in its own praise, "To spare the conquered and subdue the proud."[58] That is why, when the plan of this work requires it and as the opportunity arises, I must also speak of the earthly city—the city which, when it seeks dominion, even though whole peoples are its slaves, is itself under the dominion of its very lust for domination.

Book XV: Augustine Explains the Origins of the Two Different Cities

1. Many opinions have been held, and much has been said and written, about the felicity of paradise, about paradise itself, about the life there of the first human beings, and about their sin and punishment. We too have spoken about these matters

55. Ps. 94:15.
56. Ps. 62:8.
57. James 4:6 = 1 Pet. 5:5, citing Prov. 3:34 LXX.
58. Virgil, *Aeneid* 6.853.

in the preceding books, following holy Scripture and presenting either what we read directly in Scripture or what we could draw from Scripture in accord with its authority. To pursue these issues in more detail, however, would give rise to a great number and variety of discussions that would take more volumes to unravel than this work requires or our time permits. We do not have the leisure to linger over every puzzle that might be raised by people who have time on their hands and want to go into every detail, the kind of people who are more ready to pose questions than they are capable of understanding the answers.

All the same, I think that I have already dealt adequately with the great and difficult questions concerning the beginning of the world, of the soul, and of the human race itself. We have divided the human race into two groups, one consisting of those who live according to man and the other of those who live according to God. Speaking allegorically, we also call these two groups two cities, that is, two human societies, one predestined to reign with God for all eternity, the other to undergo eternal punishment with the devil. But this is their final end, which is to be discussed later. At this point, since enough has been said about the rise of these two cities, whether in the angels, whose number is beyond our knowing, or in the two first human beings, it seems to me that I should now undertake to trace the course that each has followed from the point at which the first two human beings began to have children down to the point at which humans will cease to have children. For the course followed by the two cities that we are discussing runs through this whole period, or age, in which the dying pass away and the newborn take their place.

Cain and Abel; the Earthly City and the Heavenly City

Cain, then, was the first child born to those two parents of the human race, and he belonged to the city of men. Abel was born later, and he belonged to the city of God. Now, in the case of a single individual we find, in the words of the Apostle, that "it is not the spiritual that is first, but the animal, and then the spiritual,"[59] and that is why each one of us, since he comes from a condemned stock, is of necessity first evil and carnal due to Adam, but, if he advances by being reborn in Christ, will afterwards be good and spiritual. And it is just the same in the case of the whole human race. When those two cities began to run their course of birth and death, the first to be born was the citizen of this world, and only after him was there born the pilgrim in this world, who belonged to the city of God, predestined by grace and chosen by grace—by grace a pilgrim below and by grace a citizen above. So far as he himself is concerned, he comes from the same lump that was wholly condemned at the start; but, like a potter (and the Apostle uses this image not to be insolent but to be apt), God made from the same lump one vessel for honor and another for dishonor.[60] The vessel for dishonor, however, was made first, and then the vessel for honor. For in the individual case also, as I have already said, the unworthy comes first. That is where we have to start, but that is not where we have to stay. Afterwards comes the worthy, which we may approach by advancing towards it and where we may remain once we have reached it. It is certainly not true, then, that every evil person will be good, but it is certainly true that no one will be good who was not previously evil. And the sooner a person changes

59. 1 Cor. 15:46.
60. Rom. 9:21.

for the better, the faster he will take on the name for what he has gained and cover over the earlier term with the later one.

Scripture states, then, that Cain founded a city; but Abel, as a pilgrim, did not. For the city of the saints is on high, even though it brings forth citizens here below, in whom it is on pilgrimage until the time of its kingdom arrives. Then it will gather them all together as they rise again in their bodies, and the promised kingdom will be given to them, where, with their prince, "the king of the ages,"[61] they will reign for time without end.

The Earthly City and the Heavenly City, Born of Nature and Born of Grace

2. . . . In the earthly city, then, we find two features, one pointing to its own presence, the other serving by its presence to signify the heavenly city. What gives birth to citizens of the earthly city, however, is a nature vitiated by sin, and what gives birth to citizens of the heavenly city is grace liberating that nature from sin. Consequently, the former are called "vessels of wrath"[62] and the latter are called "vessels of mercy."[63] This is also signified in Abraham's two sons. For one of them, Ishmael, was born of the slave named Hagar according to the flesh; and the other, Isaac, was born of Sarah, the free woman, according to the promise. Both sons, obviously enough, came from Abraham's seed, but the one was begotten in the ordinary way, showing how nature works, while the other was given by the promise, signifying divine grace. In the one case, human practice is displayed; in the other, divine beneficence is acclaimed.

61. 1 Tim. 1:17.
62. Rom. 9:22.
63. Rom. 9:23.

3. Sarah, plainly, was barren, and in her despair of having children, she wanted at least to have from her slave what she realized that she could not have from herself. So she gave her slave to be made pregnant by her husband, with whom she had wanted to have children herself but could not. In this way, then, she exacted her due from her husband, exercising her own right in another's womb. Ishmael was born, therefore, in the ordinary human way, by sexual intercourse according to the regular course of nature. That is why it says that he "was born according to the flesh."[64] It is not that such things are not benefits that come from God, or that they are not the work of God, whose creative wisdom "reaches mightily," as Scripture says, "from one end to the other, and arranges all things sweetly."[65] But when it was a matter of signifying an unmerited gift of God, freely bestowed on humankind by divine grace, it was right for a son to be given in a manner that did not follow the usual course of nature. For nature denies children to the kind of sexual intercourse of husband and wife that was possible for Abraham and Sarah at their age; and besides, because Sarah was barren, she was not even able to have children when the root of the problem was not that she had passed the age of fertility but that she lacked the fertility appropriate to her age.

The fact that no fruit of posterity was owed to a nature in this condition signifies, then, that human nature—vitiated by sin and therefore justly condemned—did not deserve any true happiness for the future. Thus Isaac, who was born through the promise, is rightly taken to signify the children of grace, who are citizens of the free city and who share in eternal peace, where there is no love for one's personal and, so to say,

64. Gal. 4:23.
65. Wisd. of Sol. 8:1.

private will, but rather a love that rejoices in the common and immutable good and joins many hearts into one, namely, a love which is perfectly at one in the obedience of charity.

The Goods of the Earthly City and the Conflicts to Which They Give Rise

4. The earthly city, in contrast, will not be everlasting, for when it is condemned to its final punishment, it will no longer be a city. It has its good here on earth, and its joy—such joy as can be had from things of this sort—comes from sharing in this good. And, since its good is not the sort of good that brings no anxieties to those who love it, the earthly city is often divided against itself by lawsuits, wars, and conflicts, and by seeking victories that either bring death or are themselves doomed to be short-lived. For if any part of it rises up in war against another part, it seeks to be the victor over nations when it is itself the prisoner of its vices; and if, when it triumphs, it is puffed up with pride, its victory brings death. But if it takes the human condition and all its vicissitudes into account, and is more distressed by the adversities that may occur than elated by its present prosperity, then its victory is at best short-lived. For it will not be able to rule for long over those whom it was able to subdue in the moment of victory.

It would be wrong, however, to say that the things which this city desires are not goods; for even this city, in its own human fashion, is better when it has them. For it desires a sort of earthly peace for the sake of the lowest goods, and it is that peace which it wants to achieve by waging war. For if it triumphs and there is no one left to resist it, there will be peace, which the opposing parties did not have so long as they were fighting each other, in their wretched need, over things that they could not both possess at the same time. It is for this peace that grueling wars are fought, and it is this peace that supposedly glorious victory obtains.

And when the victory goes to those who were fighting for the more just cause, who can doubt that the victory deserves to be celebrated or that the resulting peace is very much to be desired? These are goods, and they are undoubtedly gifts from God. But if the higher goods are neglected, which belong to the city on high, where victory will be secure in supreme and eternal peace, and if these lower goods are desired so much that people believe them to be the only goods or love them more than the goods that they believe to be higher, then misery will necessarily follow, and their previous misery will only be made worse.

5. So it is that the first founder of the earthly city was a fratricide; for, overcome by envy, he killed his own brother, who was a citizen of the eternal city on pilgrimage on this earth. It is no wonder, then, that this first example—or archetype, as the Greeks call it—was reflected by an image of the same kind at the founding, long afterwards, of the city that was to be the head of the earthly city of which we are speaking and which was to rule over so many peoples. There also, as one of the poets says in telling of the crime, "the first walls dripped with a brother's blood."[66] For this is how Rome was founded when, as Roman history attests, Remus was killed by his brother Romulus. These two, however, were both citizens of the earthly city. Both wanted the glory of founding the Roman republic, but, as cofounders, they could not both have as much glory as only one would have as the single founder of Rome. For the rule of anyone wishing to glory in his own

66. Lucan, *Pharsalia* 1.95.

dominion would obviously be less if his power were diminished by the presence of a living co-ruler. Therefore, in order for one to have total domination, his colleague was removed, and what would have been kept smaller and better by innocence grew into something larger and worse by crime.

In contrast, the brothers Cain and Abel did not both have the same desire for earthly gains. Nor did the one who killed the other feel envious of his brother because his own dominion would be restricted if they both held rule at once, for Abel did not want to have dominion in the city founded by his brother. Cain's envy was rather the diabolical envy that the evil feel toward the good simply because they are good, while they themselves are evil. For a person's possession of the good is by no means diminished when another comes or continues to share in it. On the contrary, goodness is a possession that spreads out more and more widely insofar as those who share it are united in undivided love. In fact, anyone who is unwilling to share this possession will find that he does not possess it at all, but, the more he is able to love the one who shares it with him, the greater he will find that his own possession of it becomes.

Book XIX: Earthly Peace and the Two Cities

17. But a household of people who do not live by faith pursues an earthly peace based on the goods and advantages of this temporal life. In contrast, a household of people who live by faith looks to the eternal goods which are promised for the future. It makes use of earthly and temporal things like a pilgrim. It is not captivated by them, nor is it deflected by them from the path that leads toward God, but it is sustained by them so that it may more easily bear the burdens of the

corruptible body that weighs down the soul and may at least keep those burdens from getting any worse. Thus, use of the things necessary to this mortal life is common to both kinds of people and to both kinds of household, but each uses them for its own very different end.

So also the earthly city, which does not live by faith, seeks an earthly peace, and it establishes a concord of command and obedience among its citizens in order to bring about a kind of accommodation among human wills with regard to the things that pertain to this mortal life. And the heavenly city—or, rather, that part of it which is on pilgrimage in this mortal existence and which lives by faith—must of necessity make use of this peace as well, at least until this mortal existence, for which such peace is necessary, passes away. Consequently, for as long as it leads its pilgrim life as a captive, so to speak, in the earthly city, even though it has already received the promise of redemption and the gift of the Spirit as a pledge of that redemption, it does not hesitate to obey the laws of the earthly city, by which the things needed for sustaining this mortal life are administered. For since this mortal existence is common to both cities, its obedience serves to maintain a concord between the two with regard to the things that pertain to our mortal life.

But the earthly city has included among its members certain wise men whose views the divine teaching rejects, and these thinkers, due either to their own surmise or to demonic deception, believed that there are many gods whose favor must be gained in human affairs and that various matters fall under the various areas of responsibility that these gods are presumed to have. Thus, the body falls to one god, the mind to another; and, within the body itself, the head falls to one god, the neck to another, and each of the other parts to other gods. Similarly, within the mind, native intelligence falls to one god, learning to another, anger to another, and desire to another. And so on with regard to all the things that bear on our lives: livestock falls to one god, grain falls to another, wine to another, oil to another, woods to another, money to another, navigation to another, wars and victories to another, marriage to another, birth and fertility to another, and so on and so forth. In contrast, the heavenly city knew that the one God is alone to be worshiped, and it insisted with faithful devotion that only this God is to be served with the service which in Greek is called *latreia* and which is due only to God. As a result of this difference, it has been impossible for the heavenly city to have laws of religion in common with the earthly city. Instead, it has of necessity had to dissent from the earthly city at this point and to become an annoyance to those who think differently. As a result it has had to endure their wrath, their hatred, and the assaults of their persecutions, except when it turned back the minds of its foes, sometimes due to their fear of its sheer numbers and always due to God's aid.

So long as this heavenly city is a pilgrim on earth, then, it calls forth citizens from all peoples and gathers together a pilgrim society of all languages. It cares nothing about any differences in the manners, laws, and institutions by which earthly peace is achieved or maintained. But it does not rescind or abolish any of these; rather, it preserves and follows them, provided only that they do not interfere with the religion which teaches that we are to worship the one supreme and true God; for, however different they may be in different nations, they all aim at one and the same thing: earthly peace. Thus, even the heavenly city makes use of earthly peace during its pilgrimage, and, so far as sound piety and religion allow, it defends and seeks an accommodation among human wills with regard to the things that pertain to humanity's mortal nature. At the same time, however, it directs this earthly peace toward the heavenly peace which is so truly peace that, strictly speaking, it alone is to be considered and called the peace of the rational creature, namely, a perfectly ordered and wholly concordant fellowship in the enjoyment of God and of each other in God. When we reach this peace, our life will not be mortal but rather fully and definitely alive, and our body will not be the animal body which, so long as it is corrupted, weighs down the soul, but rather the spiritual body, in need of nothing and wholly subject to the will. So long as the heavenly city is on pilgrimage, it has this peace in faith, and by this faith it lives justly when it directs toward the attainment of this peace every good act it performs for God and—since the life of a city is most certainly social—for neighbor.

Two Cities from Two Loves

28. Two loves, then, have made two cities. Love of self, even to the point of contempt for God, made the earthly city; and love of God, even to the point of contempt for self, made the heavenly city. Thus the former glories in itself, and the latter glories in the Lord. The former seeks its glory from men, but the latter finds its highest glory in God, the witness of our conscience. The former lifts up its head in its own glory; the latter says to its God, "My glory, and the one who lifts up my head."[67] In the former the lust for domination dominates both its princes and the nations that it subjugates; in the latter both leaders and followers serve one another in love, the leaders by their counsel, the followers by their obedience. The former

67. Ps. 3:3.

loves its own strength, displayed in its men of power; the latter says to its God, "I love you, O Lord, my strength."[68]

In the former, then, its wise men, who live according to man, have pursued the goods either of the body or of their own mind or of both together; or, at best, any who were able to know God "did not honor him as God or give thanks to him, but they became futile in their thinking, and their foolish heart was darkened. Claiming to be wise"—that is, exalting themselves in their own wisdom, under the domination of pride—"they became fools; and they changed the glory of the incorruptible God into the likeness of an image of a corruptible man or of birds or of four-footed beasts or of serpents"—for in adoring idols of this kind they were either leaders or followers of the people—"and worshiped and served the creature rather than the creator, who is blessed forever."[69] In the latter, in contrast, there is no human wisdom except the piety which rightly worships the true God and which looks for its reward in the company of the saints, that is, in the company of both holy men and holy angels, "in order that God may be all in all."[70]

68. Ps. 18:1.
69. Rom. 1:21-23, 25.
70. 1 Cor. 15:28.

4

Trajectories, East and West

XIV. Gelasius, *Duo Sunt*. Letter to Emperor Anastasius (494 CE)

Gelasius I was bishop of Rome from 492 to 496 CE. This period was marked both by an increasing Western emphasis on the authority of this office, and with continued struggles with both the patriarch of Constantinople and the Roman Emperor Anastasius I. The latter, like many Eastern Christians, held to a miaphysite position—the emphasis on Christ's divinity and humanity being united into one nature. Gelasius I and the Western churches by contrast affirmed the Chalcedonian formula of the distinct preservation of both natures. Gelasius' letter insists upon the distinction between worldly and spiritual authority, claiming the latter as his own and as superior to that of the emperor.

There are two powers, august Emperor, by which this world is chiefly ruled, namely, the sacred authority of the priests and the royal power. Of these that of the priests is the more weighty, since they have to render an account for even the kings of men in the divine judgment. You are also aware, dear son, that while you are permitted honorably to rule over humankind, yet in things divine you bow your head humbly before the leaders of the clergy and await from their hands the means of your salvation. In the reception and proper disposition of the heavenly mysteries you recognize that you should be subordinate rather than superior to the religious order, and that in these matters you depend on their judgment rather than wish to force them to follow your will.

If the ministers of religion, recognizing the supremacy granted you from heaven in matters affecting the public order, obey your laws, lest otherwise they might obstruct the course of secular affairs by irrelevant considerations, with what readiness should you not yield them obedience to whom is assigned the dispensing of the sacred mysteries of religion. Accordingly, just as there is no slight danger in the case of the priests if they refrain from speaking when the service of the divinity requires, so there is no little risk for those who disdain—which God forbid—when they should obey. And if it is fitting that the hearts of the faithful should submit to all priests in general who properly administer divine affairs, how much the more is obedience due to the bishop of that see which the Most High ordained to be above all others, and which is consequently dutifully honored by the devotion of the whole church.

Bibliography

Primary Sources

Acta Martyrum Scilitanorum. In *Acta Martyrum Scilitanorum Graece edita*. Edited by Hermann Usener. Bonn, 1881.

Ambrose. "Epistula 51 (5): *Augustissimo Imperatori Theodosio*." Columns 1209–14 in *Sancti Ambrosii, Mediolanensis episcopi: Opera omnia*. Edited by J. P. Migne. Patrologia Latina 16. Paris, 1880.

____. "Epistula 72 (17)." Pages 63–69 in J. H. W. G. Liebeschuetz, *Ambrose of Milan: Political Letters and Speeches*. Liverpool: Liverpool University Press, 2005.

____. "Epistula 76 (20)." Pages 161–73 in J. H. W. G. Liebeschuetz, *Ambrose of Milan: Political Letters and Speeches*. Liverpool: Liverpool University Press, 2005.

Augustine of Hippo. "*De civitate Dei, contra paganos*." Pages 1–2 in *The Works of Saint Augustine: A Translation for the 21st Century*, Part I vol. 6: *The City of God*. Edited and translated by William Babcock. Hyde Park, NY: New City, 2012.

____. "*De civitate Dei, contra paganos*." Pages 136–43 and 374–75 in *The Works of Saint Augustine: A Translation for the 21st Century*, Part I vol. 7: *The City of God*. Edited and translated by William Babcock. Hyde Park, NY: New City, 2013.

Codex Theodosianus. Pages 440, 447–48, 456–57, 463–65, 467–68, 472, and 475 in *The Theodosian Code and Novels and the Sirmondian Constitutions: A Translation with Commentary, Glossary, and Bibliography*. Edited and translated by Clyde Pharr. Union City, NJ: Lawbook Exchange, 2001.

Ephrem Syrus. "Hymn No. 3 against Julian." Pages 243–48 in *Ephrem the Syrian: Hymns*. Translated by Kathleen E. McVey. Mahwah, NJ: Paulist, 1989.

Eusebius Pamphili. "*Historia ecclesiastica.*" Columns 882–83 and 904 in *Eusebii Pamphili, Caesareae Palaestinae episcopi: Opera omnia quae exstant*. Edited by J. P. Migne. Patrologia Graeca 20. Paris, 1857.

____. "*Vita Constantini.*" Pages 79–82, 125–26, 133–35, 177–79, and 182 in *Eusebius: Life of Constantine*. Translated with an introduction and commentary by Averil Cameron and Stuart Hall. Oxford: Clarendon, 1999.

Gelasius I. *Duo Sunt*. Pages 72–73 in *Readings in European History*. Translated by J. H. Robinson. Boston: Ginn, 1905.

Justin Martyr. "First Apology." Pages 33–34, 42–45, 52, and 107–8 in *Saint Justin Martyr: The First Apology; the Second Apology; Dialogue with Trypho; Exhortation to the Greeks; Discourse to the Greeks; the Monarchy, or the Rule of God*. Edited and translated by Thomas B. Falls. The Fathers of the Church 6. Washington, DC: Catholic University of America Press, 1965.

Libanius. "Oratio 30: *Pro templis.*" pages 100–151 in *Selected Orations*, vol. 2. Edited and translated by A. F. Norman. Loeb Classical Library 452. Cambridge, MA: Harvard University Press, 1977.

Pliny. "Letter to Trajan (Ep. 10, 96)." Pages 284–90 in Letters and Panegyrics. Translated by Betty Radice. Loeb Classical Library 2. Cambridge, MA: Harvard University Press, 1959.

____. "Rescript of Trajan on Trials of Christians (Ep. 10, 97)." Pages 290–92 in Letters and Panegyrics. Translated by Betty Radice. Loeb Classical Library 2. Cambridge, MA: Harvard University Press, 1959.

Symmachus. "Relatio III." Pages 71–78 in J. H. W. G. Liebeschuetz, *Ambrose of Milan: Political Letters and Speeches*. Liverpool: Liverpool University Press, 2005.

Tertullian. "Apologeticum (28:3–33:4): *Apologeticus adversus gentes pro christianis*." Pages 140–44 in *Opera*, Part I: *Opera catholica:* Adversus Marcionem. Edited by E. Kroymann. Corpus christianorum, series Latina 1. Turnhout: Brepols, 1954.

Theodoret. "*Historia ecclesiastica*." Columns 1231–37 in *Theodoreti, Cyrensis episcopi: Opera omnia*. Edited by J. P. Migne. Patrologia Graeca 82. Paris, 1875.

Secondary Sources

Barnes, Timothy David. *Constantine and Eusebius*. Cambridge, MA and London: Harvard University Press, 1981.

Brown, Peter. *Augustine: A Biography. A New Edition with an Epilogue.* Berkeley and Los Angeles: University of California Press, 2000.

Burns, James Henderson. *The Cambridge History of Medieval Political Thought, c. 350-c. 1450*. Cambridge: Cambridge University Press, 1988.

Cameron, Averil. *Christianity and the Rhetoric of Empire: The Development of Christian Discourse.* Berkeley and Los Angeles: University of California Press, 1991.

____. *The Later Roman Empire: AD 284–430*. Cambridge, MA: Harvard University Press, 1993.

____. *The Mediterranean World in Late Antiquity, 395–700 A.D.* London and New York: Routledge, 2015.

Cribiore, Raffaela. *The School of Libanius in Late Antique Antioch.* Princeton and Oxford: Princeton University Press, 2007.

Daniélou, Jean, and Henri Marrou. *The First Six Hundred Years*, vol. 1: *The Christian Centuries*. Edited by L. J. Rogier, R. Aubert, and M. D.

Knowles. Translated by Vincent Cronin. New York: McGraw-Hill, 1964.

Field, Lester. *Liberty, Dominion, and the Two Swords: On the Origins of Western Political Theology (180–398).* South Bend, IN: University of Notre Dame Press, 1998.

Frend, W. H. D. "Open Questions Concerning the Christians and the Roman Empire in the Age of the Severi," *Journal of Theological Studies* 25 (1974): 331–51.

Harvey, Susan Ashbrook, and David Hunter, eds. *The Oxford Handbook of Early Christian Studies.* Oxford: Oxford University Press, 2008.

Kalantzis, George. *Caesar and the Lamb: Early Christian Attitudes on War and Military Service.* Eugene, OR: Cascade, 2012.

Lenski, Noel, ed. *Cambridge Companion to the Age of Constantine.* Cambridge: Cambridge University Press, 2012.

Liebeschuetz, J. H. W. G. *Ambrose of Milan: Political Letters and Speeches.* Liverpool: Liverpool University Press, 2005.

McLynn, Neil B. *Ambrose of Milan: Church and Court in a Christian Capital.* Berkeley and Los Angeles: University of California Press, 1994.

O'Donnell, James J. *Augustine: A New Biography.* New York: HarperCollins, 2006.

Pelikan, Jaroslav J. *The Christian Tradition*, vol. 1: *The Emergence of the Catholic Tradition.* Chicago: University of Chicago Press, 1971.

Rapp, Claudia. *Holy Bishops in Late Antiquity: The Nature of Christian Leadership in an Age of Transition.* Berkeley and Los Angeles: University of California Press, 2005.

Rousseau, Philip, ed. *A Companion to Late Antiquity.* Hoboken, NJ: Wiley, 2012.

Uhalde, Kevin. *Expectations of Justice in the Age of Augustine.* Philadelphia: University of Pennsylvania Press, 2013.

Wilken, Robert. *The First Thousand Years: A Global History of Christianity.* New Haven and London: Yale University Press, 2012.

Index